Andrew Lang

Lost leaders

Andrew Lang

Lost leaders

ISBN/EAN: 9783743320536

Manufactured in Europe, USA, Canada, Australia, Japa

Cover: Foto ©ninafisch / pixelio.de

Manufactured and distributed by brebook publishing software (www.brebook.com)

Andrew Lang

Lost leaders

CONTENTS.

	PAGE
SCOTCH RIVERS	1
SALMON-FISHING	9
WINTER SPORTS	17
HUMAN LEVITATION	24
A CHINAMAN'S MARRIAGE	31
SIEUR DE MONTAIGNE	38
THACKERAY'S DRAWINGS	45
GOLF	53
ART OF DINING	62
AMERICAN HUMOUR	70
SUSPENDED ANIMATION	78
BREAKING UP	85
ON SHAVING	92
STREET NOISES	100
LENDING OF BOOKS	107
CLUB BORES	114
PHIZ ...	121

CONTENTS

	PAGE
Theory and Practice of Proposals	128
Master Samuel Pepys	135
Involuntary Bailees	143
Summer Nights	150
On Hypochondriacs	158
Thackeray's London	166
Torrid Summer	173
Western Drolls	181
Show Sunday	189
The Dry Fly	197
Amateur Authors	204
Some Rare Things for Sale	211
Curiosity Hunting	219

LOST LEADERS.

SCOTCH RIVERS.

SEPTEMBER is the season of the second and lovelier youth of the river-scenery of Scotland. Spring comes but slowly up that way; it is June before the woods have quite clothed themselves. In April the angler or the sketcher is chilled by the east wind, whirling showers of hail, and even when the river-banks are sweet with primroses, the bluff tops of the border hills are often bleak with late snow. This state of things is less unpropitious to angling than might be expected. A hardy race of trout will sometimes rise freely to the artificial fly when the natural fly is destroyed, and the angler is almost blinded with dusty snowflakes. All through mid-summer the Scotch rivers lose their chief attractions. The bracken has not yet changed its green for the fairy gold, the hue of its decay; the woods wear a uniform and sombre green; the waters are low and shrunken, and angling is almost impossible. But with September the pleasant season returns for people who love "to be quiet, and go a-fishing," or a-sketching. The hills put on a wonderful harmony of colours, the woods rival the October splendours of English forests. The bends of the Tweed below Melrose and round Mertoun—a scene that, as Scott says, the river seems loth to leave— may challenge comparison with anything the Thames can show at Nuneham or Cliefden. The angler, too, is as fortunate as the lover of the picturesque. The trout that have hidden themselves all summer, or at best have cautiously nibbled at the worm-bait, now rise freely to the fly. Wherever a yellow leaf drops from birch tree or elm the great trout are splashing, and they are too eager to distinguish very subtly between flies of nature's making and flies of fur and feather. It is a time when every one who can manage it should be by the water-side, and should take with him, if possible, the posthumous

work of Sir Thomas Dick Lauder on the
" Rivers of Scotland."

This book, as the author of " Rab and
his Friends" tells us in the preface, is a re-
publication of articles written in 1848, on
the death-bed of the author, a man of
many accomplishments and of a most lovable
nature. He would lie and dictate or write
in pencil these happy and wistful memories
of days passed by the banks of Tweed and
Tyne. He did not care to speak of the
northern waters: of Tay, which the Roman
invaders compared to Tiber ; of Laxford, the
river of salmon ; or of the "thundering Spey."
Nor has he anything to say of the west, and
of Galloway, the country out of which young
Lochinvar came, with its soft and broken
hills, like the lower spurs of the Pyrenees,
and its streams, now rushing down defiles
of rock, now stealing with slow foot through
the plains. He confines himself to the limits
of the Scottish Arcadia ; to the hills near
Edinburgh, where Ramsay's Gentle Shepherd
loved and sang in a rather affected way ; and
to the main stream and the tributaries of the
Tweed. He tells, with a humour like that of
Charles Lamb in his account of his youthful

search for the mysterious fountain-head of the New River, how he sought among the Pentland Hills for the source of the brook that flowed past his own garden. The wandering stream led him through many a scene renowned in Border history, up to the heights whence Marmion surveyed the Scottish forces encamped on Borough Moor before the fatal day of Flodden. These scenes are described with spirit and loving interest; but it is by Tweedside that the tourist will find his most pleasant guide in Lauder's book. Just as Cicero said of Athens, that in every stone you tread on a history, so on Tweedside by every nook and valley you find the place of a ballad, a story, or a legend. From Tweed's source, near the grave of the Wizard Merlin, down to Berwick and the sea, the Border "keeps" and towers are as frequent as castles on the Rhine. Each has its tradition, its memory of lawless times, which have become beautiful in the magic of poetry and the mist of the past. First comes Neidpath Castle, with its vaulted "hanging chamber" in the roof, and the rafter, with the iron ring to which prisoners were hanged, still remaining to testify to the lawless power of Border lords.

Neidpath has a softer legend of the death of the lady of the house, when her lover failed to recognize the features that had wasted with sorrow for his absence. Lower down the river comes Clovenfords, with its memories of Christopher North, and Peebles, where King James I. sings that there was "dancing and derray" in his time; and still lower Ashiesteel, where Scott was young and happy, and Abbotsford, where his fame and his misfortunes found him out. It was on a bright afternoon in late September that he died there, and the mourners by his bed heard through the silence the murmuring of Tweed. How many other associations there are by the tributary rivers! what a breath of "pastoral melancholy"! There is Ettrick, where the cautious lover in the old song of Ettrick banks found "a canny place of meeting." Oakwood Tower, where Michael Scott, the wizard, wove his spells, is a farm building— the haunted magician's room is a granary; Earlstone, where Thomas the Rhymer dwelt, and whence the two white deer recalled him to Elfland and to the arms of the fairy queen, is noted "for its shawl manufactory." Only Yarrow still keeps its ancient quiet, and the burn that was tinged by the blood of Douglas is unstained by more commonplace dyes.

All these changes make the "Rivers of Scotland" rather melancholy reading. Thirty years have not passed since Lauder died, and how much he would miss if he could revisit his beloved water! Spearing salmon by torchlight is a forbidden thing. The rocks are no longer lit up with the red glow; they resound no longer with the shouts and splashing of the yeomen. You might almost as readily find a hart on Harthope, or a wild cat at Catslack, or a wolf at Wolf-Cleugh, as catch three stone-weight of trout in Meggatwater.* The days of guileless fish and fabulous draughts of trout are over. No sportsman need take three large baskets to the Gala now, as Lauder did, and actually filled them with thirty-six dozen of trout. The modern angler must not allow his expectations to be raised too highly by these stories. Sport has become much more difficult in these times of rapidly growing population. It is a pleasant sight to see the weavers spending their afternoons beside the Tweed;

---

* Except with worm in a summer flood.

it is such a sight as could not be witnessed by the closely preserved rivers of England. But the weavers have taught the trout caution, and the dyes and various pollutions of trade have thinned their numbers. Mr. Ruskin sees no hope in this state of things; he preaches, in the spirit of old Hesiod, that there is no piety in a race which defiles the "holy waters." But surely civilization, even if it spoil sport and degrade scenery, is better than a state of things in which the laird would hang up his foes to an iron ring in the roof. The hill of Cowden Knowes may be a less eligible place for lovers' meetings than it was of old. But in those times the lord of Cowden Knowes is said by tradition to have had a way of putting his prisoners in barrels studded with iron nails, and rolling them down a brae. This is the side of the good old times which should not be overlooked. It may not be pleasant to find blue dye and wool yarn in Teviot, but it is more endurable than to have to encounter the bandit Barnskill, who hewed his bed of flint, Scott says, in Minto Crags. Still, the reading of the "Rivers of Scotland" leaves rather a sad impression on the reader, and makes him ask once more if there is no way of reconciling the beauty of rude ages with the comforts and culture of civilization. This is a question that really demands an answer, though it is often put in a mistaken way. The teachings of Mr. Ruskin and of his followers would bring us back to a time when printing was not, and an engineer would have been burned for a wizard.* But there is a point at which civilization and production must begin to respect the limits of the beautiful, on which they so constantly encroach. Who is to settle the limit, and escape the charge of being either a *dilettante* and a sentimentalist on the one hand, or a Philistine on the other?

* Perhaps an Editor put this moral in?

SALMON-FISHING.

SALMON-FISHING for this season is over, and, in spite of the fresh and open weather, most anglers will feel that the time has come to close the fly-book, to wind up the reel, and to consign the rod to its winter quarters. Salmon-fishing ceases to be very enjoyable when the *snaw broo*, or melted snow from the hilltops, begins to mix with the brown waters of Tweed or Tay; when the fallen leaves hamper the hook; and when the fish are becoming sluggish, black, and the reverse of comely. Now the season of retrospect commences, the time of the pleasures of memory, and the delights of talking shop dear to anglers. Most sporting talk is dull to every one but the votaries of the particular amusement. Few things can be drearier to the outsider than the conversation of cricketers, unless it be the recondite lore which whist-players bring forth from the depths of their extraordinary memories. But angling talk has a variety, recounts an amount of incident and adventure, and wakens a feeling of free air in a way with which the records of no other sport, except perhaps deer-stalking, can compete. The salmon is, beyond all rivalry, the strongest and most beautiful, and most cautious and artful, of fresh-water fishes. To capture him is not a task for slack muscles or an uncertain eye. There is even a slight amount of personal risk in the sport. The fisher must often wade till the water reaches above the waist in cold and rushing streams, where his feet are apt to slip on the smooth stones or trip on the rough rocks beneath him. When the salmon takes the fly, there is no time for picking steps. The line rushes out so swiftly as to cut the fingers if it touches them, and then is the moment when the angler must follow the fish at the top of his speed. To stand still, or to go cautiously in pursuit, is to allow the salmon to run out with an enormous length of line; the line is submerged—technically speaking, *drowned*—in the water, the strain of the supple rod is removed from the fish, who finds the hook loose in his mouth, and rubs it off against the bottom of the river. Thus speed of foot, in water or over rocks, is a necessary quality in the angler; at least in the northern angler. By the banks of the Usk a contemplative man who likes to take things easily may find pretty sure footing on grassy slopes, or on a gravelly bottom. But it is a different thing to hook a large salmon where the Tweed foams under the bridge of Yair down to the narrows and linns below. If the angler hesitates there, he is lost. Does he stand still and give the fish line? The astute creature cuts it against the sharp rocks below the bridge, and the rod, relieved of the weight, leaps straight in the fisher's hand, and in his heart there is a sense of emptiness and sudden desolation. Does he try to follow, the chances are that his feet slip; after one or two wild struggles he is on his back in the water, and nearly strangled with his fishing-basket. In either case the fish goes on his way rejoicing, and, after the manner of his kind, leaps out of the water once or twice—a maddening sight.

Adventures like this are among the bitter memories of the angler. The fish that break away are monstrous animals; imagination increases their bulk, and fond desire paints them clean-run and bright as silver. There are other chances of the angler's life scarcely less sad than this. When a hook breaks just as the salmon was losing strength, was ceasing to struggle, and beginning to sway with the mere force of the stream, and to show his shining sides—when a hook breaks at such a moment, it is very hard to bear. The oath of Ernulphus seems all too weak to express the feelings of the sportsman and his wrath against the wretched tackle-maker. Again, when the fish is actually conquered; when he is being towed gently into some little harbour among the tall slim water-grasses, or into a pebbly cove, or up to a green bank; when the bitterness of struggle is past, and he seems resigned and almost happy; when at this crisis the clumsy gilly with the gaff scratches him, rouses him to a last exertion, and entangles the line, so that the salmon breaks free—that is an experience to which language cannot do justice. The ancient painter drew his veil over the face of Agamemnon present at his daughter's sacrifice. Silence and sympathy are all one can offer to the angler who has toiled all day, and in this wise caught nothing. There is yet another very bitter sorrow. It is a hard thing for a man to leave town and hurry to a river in the west, a river that perhaps he has known since he fished for minnows with a bent pin in happy childhood. The west is not a dry land; effeminate tourists complain that the rain it raineth every day. But the heavy soft rain is the very life of an angler. It keeps the stream of that clear brown hue, between porter and amber, which he loves; and it encourages the salmon to keep rushing from the estuary and the sea right up to the mountain loch, where they rest. But suppose there is a dry summer—and such things have been even in Argyleshire. The heart of the tourist is glad within him, but as the river shrinks and shrinks, a silver thread among slimy green mosses in the streams, a sheet of clear water in the pools, the angler repines. Day after sultry day goes by, and there is no hope. There is a cloud on the distant hill; it is only the smoke from some moor that has caught fire. The river grows so transparent that it is easy to watch the lazy fish sulking at the bottom. Then comes a terrible temptation. Men, men calling themselves sportsmen, have been known to fish in the innocent dewy morning, with worm, with black lob worm. Worse remains behind. Persons of ungoverned passions, maddened by the sight of the fish, are believed to have poached with rake-hooks, a cruel apparatus made of three hooks fastened back to back and loaded with lead. These are thrown over the fish, and then struck into him with a jerk. But the mind willingly turns away from the contemplation of such actions.

It is pleasanter to think of not unsuccessful days by lowland or highland streams, when the sun was veiled, the sky pearly grey, the water, as the people say, in grand order. There is the artistic excitement of choosing the hook, gaudy for a heavy water, neat and modest for a clearer stream. There is the feverish moment of adjusting rod and line, while you mark a fish "rising to himself." You begin to cast well above him, and come gradually down, till the fly lights on the place where he is lying. Then there is a slow pull, a break in the water, a sudden strain at the line, which flies through the rings of the rod. It is not well to give too much line; best to follow his course, as he makes off as if for Berwick and the sea. Once or twice he leaps clean into the air, a flying bar of silver. Then he sulks at the bottom, a mere dead weight, attempting devices only to be conjectured. A common plan now is to tighten the line, and tap the butt end of the rod. This humane expedient produces effects not unlike neuralgia, it may be supposed, for the fish is off in a new fury. But rush after rush grows tamer, till he is drawn within reach of the gaff, and so on to the grassy bed, where a tap on the head ends his sorrows, and the colours on his shining side undulate in delicate and beautiful radiance. It may be dreadfully cruel, as cruel as nature and human life; but those who eat salmon or butcher's meat cannot justly protest, for they, desiring the end, have willed the means. As the angler walks home, and watches the purple Eildon grow grey in the twilight, or sees the hills of Mull delicately outlined between the faint gold of sky and sea, it is not probable that his conscience reproaches him very fiercely. He has spent a day among the most shy and hidden beauties of nature, surprising her here and there in places where, unless he had gone a-fishing, he might never have penetrated. He has set his skill against the strength and skill of the monarch of rivers, and has mastered him among the haunts of fairies and beneath the ruined towers of feudalism. These are some of the delights that to-day end for a season.*

* The author once caught a salmon. It did not behave in any way like the ferocious fish in this article.

WINTER SPORTS.

PEOPLE to whom cold means misery, who hate to be braced, and shudder at the word "seasonable," can have little difficulty in accounting for the origin of the sports of winter. They need only adapt to the circumstances that old Lydian tradition which says that games of chance were invented during a great famine. Men permitted themselves to eat only every second day, and tried to forget their hunger in playing at draughts and dice. That is clearly the invention of a southern people, which never had occasion to wish it could become oblivious of the weather, as too many of us would like to be in England. Such shivering and indolent folks may be inclined to say that skating and curling and wildfowl-shooting, and the other diversions which seduce the able-bodied from the warm precincts of the cheerful fire, were only contrived to enable us to forget the state of the thermometer. Whether or not that was the purpose of the first northerner who fixed sheep-bones beneath his feet, to course more smoothly over the frozen sound, there can be no doubt that winter sports answer their presumed purpose. They keep up that glow which only exercise in the open air can give, and promote the health which shows itself in the complexion. It is the young lady who interprets literally the Scotch invitation "come into the fire," and who spoils the backs of library novels by holding them too near the comfortable hearth, she it is who suffers from the ignoble and unbecoming liberties that winter takes with the human countenance. Happier and wiser is she who studies the always living and popular Dutch roll rather than the Grecian bend, and who blooms with continual health and good temper. Our changeful climate affords so few opportunities of learning to skate, that it is really extraordinary to find so much skill, and to see feats so difficult and graceful. In Canada, where frost is a certainty, and where the covered "rinks" make skating an indoor sport, it is not odd that great perfection should be attained. But as fast as Canadians bring over a new figure or a new trick it is picked up, and critics may dispute as to whether the bold and dashing style of the English school of skaters is not preferable to the careful and smooth, but somewhat pretty and niggling manner of the colonists. Our skating stands to the Canadian fashion somewhat as French does to English etching. We have the dash and the *chic* with skates which Frenchmen show with the etching-needle, and the Canadian, on the other hand, is apt to decline into the mere prettiness which is th fault of English etchers.

Skating has been, within the last few years, a very progressive art. There was a time when mere speed, and the grace of speed, satisfied most amateurs. The ideal spot for skating in those days must have been the lakes where Wordsworth used to listen to the echoes replying from the cold and moonlit hills, or such a frozen river as that on which the American skater was pursued by wolves. No doubt such scenes have still their rare charm, and few expeditions are more attractive than a moonlight exploration of a winding river. But it is seldom that our frosts make such tours practicable, whereas almost every winter it is possible to skate with safety, at least on shallow ponds, or on places like the ice-bound floods at Oxford. Thus figure-skating, which needs but a surface of a few yards to each performer, has come into fashion, and it is hard to imagine any exercise more elegant, or one that requires more nerve. The novice is theoretically aware that if he throws his body into certain unfamiliar postures, which are explained to him, the laws of gravitation and of the higher curves will cause him to complete a certain figure. But how much courage and faith it requires to yield to these laws and let the frame swing round subject to the immutable rules of matter! The temptation to stop half-way is almost irresistible, and then there occurs a complicated fall, which makes the petrified spectator ask where may be the skater's body—"which are legs, and which are arms?" Of all sports, skating has the best claim to adopt Danton's motto, *Toujours de l'audace*—the audacity meant being that of giving one's self up to the laws of motion, and not the vulgar quality which carries its owner on to dangerous ice. Something may now be learned of figure-skating on dry land, and the adventure may be renewed of the mythical children who went sliding all on a summer day. In this respect, skating has a great advantage over its rival, the "roaring game" of curling. It would be poor fun to curl on asphalte, with stones fixed on wheels, though the amusement is possible, and we recommend the idea, which is not copyright, to enthusiastic curlers; and curlers are almost always enthusiastic. It is pleasant to think how the hills must be ringing with their shouts, round many a lonely tarn, where the men of one parish meet those of the next in friendly conflict north of the Tweed. The exhilarating yell of "soop her up," whereby the curler who wields a broom is abjured to sweep away the snow in front of the advancing stone, will many a time be heard this winter. There is something peculiarly healthy about this sport— in the ring with which the heavy stones clash against each other; in the voices of the burly plaided men, shepherd, and farmer, and laird; in the rough banquet of beef and greens and the copious toddy which close the day's exertions.

Frost brings with it an enforced close-season for most of furred and feathered kind. The fox is safe enough, and, if sportsmen are right, must be rather wearying for open weather, and for the return of his favourite exercise with hounds. But even when the snow hangs out her white flag of truce and goodwill between man and beast, the British sportsman is still the British sportsman, and is not averse to going out and killing something. To such a one, wild-fowl shooting is a possibility, though, as good Colonel Hawker says, some people complain forsooth that it interferes with ease and comfort. We should rather incline to think it does. A black frost with no moon is not precisely the kind of weather that a degenerate sportsman would choose for lying in the frozen mud behind a bush, or pushing a small punt set on large skates across the ice to get at birds. Few attitudes can be more cramping than that of the gunner who skulks on one knee behind his canoe, pushing it with one hand, and dragging himself along by the aid of the other. Then, it is disagreeable to have to use a gun so heavy that the stock is fitted with a horsehair pillow, or even with a small bolster. The whistle of widgeon and the shrill-sounding pinions of wild geese may be attractive noises, and no doubt all shooting is exciting; and a form of shooting which stakes all on one shot must offer some thrilling moments of expectation. The quarry has to be measured by number, not by size, and fifty widgeon at one discharge, or a brace of wild swans may almost serve to set against a stag of ten.* The lover of nature has glimpses in wild-fowl shooting such as she gives no other man—the glittering expanse of waters, the birds "all in a charm," all uttering their cry together, the musical moan of the tide, and the "long glories of the winter moon." But success is too difficult, equipment too costly, and rheumatism too certain for wild-fowl shooting to be reckoned among popular winter sports.

* Mr. Wordsworth, in his poem of "The Recluse," expresses a horror of this diversion.

HUMAN LEVITATION.

WHY is it that living fish add nothing to the "weight of the bucket of water in which they swim?" Charles II. is said to have asked the Royal Society. A still more extraordinary question has been propounded in the grave pages of the *Quarterly Journal of Science*, edited by Mr. Crookes, a Fellow of the Royal Society, and the discoverer of the useful metal thallium. The problem set in this learned review does not, like that of the Merry Monarch, beg the question of facts. "What is the scientific inference from the various accounts, modern and traditional, of human levitation?" is the difficulty before the world at this present moment. Now, there may be people who never heard of levitation, nor even of "thaums," a term that frequently occurs in the article we refer to. A slight acquaintance with the dead languages, whose shadows reappear in this queer fashion, enables the inquirer to decide that "levitation" means the power of becoming lighter than the surrounding atmosphere, and setting at nought the laws of gravitation.

Thaums, again, are wonders, and there is no very obvious reason why they should not be called wonders. But to return to levitation. Most of us have heard how Mr. Home and other gifted people possess the faculty of being raised from the ground, and of floating about the room, or even out of the window. There are clouds of witnesses who have observed these phenomena, which generally occur in the dark. In fact, they are part of that vague subject called spiritualism, about which opinion is so much divided, and views are so vague. It has been said that the human race, in regard to this high argument, is divided into five classes. There are people who believe; people who investigate; people who think the matter really ought to be looked into; people who dislike the topic, but who would believe in the phenomena if they were proved; and people of common sense, who would not believe in them if they were proved. Now, the article in the *Journal of Science* only deals with one of the phenomena we hear so much of—that of the sudden suspension of the laws of gravitation, in the case of individual men. The author has collected a vast variety of traditions bearing on this subject, and his conclusion apparently is, that events of this kind, though rather rare, are natural, are peculiar to people of certain temperament and organization, and, above all, bring no proof as to the truth of the doctrines asserted by the persons who exhibit the phenomena. Now, men of science, as a rule, and the world at large, look on stories of this sort as myths, romances, false interpretations of subjective feelings, pious frauds, and absurd nonsense. Before expressing an opinion, it may be well to look over the facts, as they are called, which are brought under our notice.

What accounts, then, are there of levitation among the civilized people of the Old World? First, there is Abaris, the Scythian, "in the time of Pythagoras," says our author. Well, as a matter of evidence, Abaris may have been levitated in the eighth century before Christ, or it may have been two hundred and fifty years later. Perhaps he was a Druid of the Hebrides. Toland thought so, and Toland had as good a chance of knowing as any one else. Our earliest authority, Herodotus, says he took no earthly food, and "went with his arrow all round the world without once eating." It seems that he rode on this arrow, which, Mr. Rawlinson thinks, may possibly have been an early tradition of the magnet. All our detailed information about him is of later date than the Christian era. The fact remains that tradition says he was able to fly in the air. Pythagoras is said to have had the same power, or rather the same faculty came upon him. He was lifted up, with no will or conscious exertion of his own. Now, our evidence as to the power of Pythagoras to be "like a bird, in two places at once," is exactly as valuable as that about Abaris. It rests on the tradition repeated by superstitious philosophers who lived eight hundred years after his death. "To Pythagoras, therefore," as Herodotus has it, "we now say farewell," with no further knowledge than that vague tradition says he was "levitated." The writer now leaves classical antiquity behind him—he does not repeat a saying of Plotinus, the mystic of Alexandria, who lived in the third century of our era. The best known anecdote of him is that his disciples asked him if he were not sometimes levitated, and he laughed, and said, "No; but he was no fool who persuaded you of this." Instead of Plotinus, we are referred to a mass of Jewish and anti-Christian apocryphal traditions, which have the same common point—the assertion of the existence of the phenomenon of levitation. Apollonius of Tyana is also said to have been a highly accomplished medium. We are next presented with a list of forty "levitated" persons, canonized or beatified by the Church of Rome. Their dates range from the ninth to the seventeenth century, and their histories go to prove that levitation runs in families. Perhaps the best known of the collection is St. Theresa (1515–1582), and it is only fair to say that the stories about St. Theresa are very like those repeated about our lady mediums. One of these, Mrs. Guppy, as every one knows, can scatter flowers all over a room, "flowers of Paradise," unknown to botanists. Fauna, rather than flora, was St. Theresa's province, and she kept a charming pet, a little white animal of no recognized species. Still, about her, and about her friend St. John of the Cross, the legend runs that they used to be raised off the ground, chairs and all, and float about in the most soothing way. Poor Peter of Alcantara was levitated in a less pleasant manner; "he uttered a frightful cry, and shot through the air as if he had been fired from a gun." Peter had a new form of epilepsy—the rising, not the falling, sickness. Joseph Copertino, again, floated about to such good effect, that in 1650 Prince John of Brunswick foreswore the Protestant faith. The logical process which converted this prince is not a very obvious one.

Why do we quote all these old monkish and neoplatonic legends? For some the evidence is obviously nil; to other anecdotes many witnesses bear testimony; but then, we know that an infectious *schwärmerei* can persuade people that the lion now removed from Northumberland House wagged his tail. The fact is that there is really matter for science in all these anecdotes, and the question to be asked is this—How does it happen that in ages and societies so distant and so various identical stories are current? What is the pressure that makes neoplatonic gossips of the fourth century circulate the same marvels as spiritualist gossips of the nineteenth?

How does it happen that the mediæval saint, the Indian medicine-man, the Siberian shaman (a suggestive term), have nearly identical wonders attributed to them? If people wanted merely to tell "a good square lie," as the American slang has it, invention does not seem to have such pitifully narrow boundaries. It appears to follow that there are contagious nervous illusions, about which science has not said the last word. We believe that the life of children, with its innocent mixture of dreams and waking, facts and fancies, could supply odd parallels to the stories we have been treated to. And as we are on the subject, we should like, as the late President Lincoln said, to tell a little story. It occurred to a learned divine to meet a pupil, who ought by rights to have been in the University of Oxford, walking in Regent Street. The youth glided past like a ghost, and was lost in the crowd; next day his puzzled preceptor received a note, dated on the previous day from Oxford, telling how the pupil had met the teacher by the Isis, and on inquiry had heard he was in London. Here is a case of levitation—of double levitation, and we leave it to be explained by the followers of Abaris and of Mr. Home.

A CHINAMAN'S MARRIAGE.

THE Court of Assizes at Paris has lately been occupied with the case of a Chinese gentleman, whose personal charms and literary powers make him worthy to be the compatriot of Ah-Sin, that astute Celestial. Tin-tun-ling is the name—we wish we could say, with Thackeray's F. B., "the highly respectable name"—of the Chinese who has just been acquitted on a charge of bigamy. In China, it is said that the more distinguished a man is the shorter is his title, and the name of a very victorious general is a mere click or gasp. On this principle, the trisyllabic Tin-tun-ling must have been without much honour in his own country. In Paris, however, he has learned Parisian aplomb, and when confronted with his judges and his accusers, his air, we learn, "was very calm." "His smile it was pensive and bland," like the Heathen

Chinee's, and his calm confidence was justified by events. It remains to tell the short, though not very simple, tale of Tin-tun-ling. Mr. Ling was born in 1831, in the province of Chan-li. At the interesting age of eighteen, an age at which the intellect awakens and old prejudices lose their grasp, he ceased to burn gilt paper on the tombs of his ancestors; he ceased to revere their august spirits; he gave up the use of the planchette, rejected the teachings of Confucius, and, in short, became a convert to Christianity. This might be considered either as a gratifying testimony to the persuasive powers of Catholic missionaries, or as an example of the wiles of Jesuitism, if we did not know the inner history of Mr. Ling's soul, the abysmal depths of his personality. He has not, like many other modern converts, written a little book, such as "How I ceased to chinchin Joss; or, from Confucius to Christianity," but he has told Madame Judith Mendès all about it. Madame Mendès has made a name in literature, and English readers may have wondered how the daughter of the poet Théophile Gautier came to acquire the knowledge of Chinese which she has shown in her translations from that language. It now appears that she was the pupil of Tin-tun-ling, who, in a moment of expansion, confided to her that he adopted the Catholic faith that he might eat a morsel of bread. He was starving, it seems; he had eaten nothing for eight days, when he threw himself on the charity of the missionaries, and received baptism. Since Winckelmann turned renegade, and became a Roman Catholic merely that the expenses of his tour to Rome and his maintenance there might be paid, there have surely been few more mercenary converts. Tin-tun-ling was not satisfied with being christened into the Church, he was also married in Catholic rites, and here his misfortunes fairly began, and he entered on the path which has led him into difficulty and discredit.

The French, as a nation, are not remarkable for their accuracy in the use of foreign proper names, and we have a difficulty in believing that the name of Mr. Ling's first wife was really Quzia-Tom-Alacer. There is a touch of M. Hugo's famous Tom Jim Jack, the British tar, about this designation. Nevertheless, the facts are that Tin-tun-ling was wedded to Quzia, and had four children by her. After years of domestic life, on which he is said to look back but rarely and with reluctance, he got a position as secretary and shoeblack and tutor in Chinese to a M. Callery, and left the province of Chin-li for Paris. For three months this devoted man sent Quzia-Tom-Alacer small sums of money, and after that his kindness became, as Douglas Jerrold said, unremitting. Quzia heard of her lord no more till she learned that he had forgotten his marriage vow, and was, in fact, Another's. As to how Tin-tun-ling contracted a matrimonial alliance in France, the evidence is a little confusing. It seems certain that after the death of his first employer, Callery, he was in destitution; that M. Théophile Gautier, with his well-known kindness and love of curiosities, took him up, and got him lessons in Chinese, and it seems equally certain that in February, 1872, he married a certain Caroline Julie Liégeois. In the act of marriage, Tin-tun-ling described himself as a baron, which we know that he was not, for in his country he did not rejoice in buttons and other insignia of Chinese nobility. As Caroline Julie Ling (*née* Liégeois) denounced her lord for bigamy in 1873, and succeeded, as has been seen, in proving that he was husband of Quzia-Tom-Alacer, it may seem likely that she found out the spurious honours of the pretended title. But whatever may be thought of the deceitful conduct of Ling, there is little doubt apparently that Caroline is really his. He stated in court that by Chinese law a husband who has not heard of his wife for three years may consider that his marriage has legally ceased to be binding. Madame Mendès proved from the volume Ta-Tsilg-Leu-Lee, the penal code of China, that Ling's law was correct. It also came out in court that Quzia-Tom-Alacer had large feet. The jury, on hearing this evidence, very naturally acquitted Tin-tun-ling, whom Madame Mendès embraced, it is said, with the natural fervour of a preserver of innocence. Whether Tin-tun-ling is now a bachelor, or whether he is irrevocably bound to Caroline Julie, is a question that seems to have occurred to no one.

The most mysterious point in this dark business is the question, How did Tin-tun-ling, who always spoke of his first marriage with terror, happen to involve himself in the difficulties of a second? Something more than the common weakness of human nature must have been at work here. Madame Mendès says, like a traitor to her sex, that Tin espoused Caroline Julie from feelings of compassion. He yielded, according to Madame Mendès, "to the entreaties of this woman." The story of M. Gustave Lafargue confirms this ungallant tale. According to M. Lafargue, Tin's bride was a governess, and an English governess, or at least one who taught English. She proposed to marry Tin, who first resisted, and then hesitated. In a matter of this kind, the man who hesitates is lost. The English governess flattered Tin's literary as well as his personal vanity. She proposed to translate the novels which Tin composes in his native tongue, and which he might expect to prove as popular in France as some other fictions of his fatherland have done in times past. So they were married. Tim, though on pleasure bent, had a frugal mind, and after a wedding-breakfast, which lasted all day, he went to a theatre to ask for two free passes. When he came back his bride was gone. He sought her with all the ardour of the bridegroom in the ballad of "The Mistletoe Bough," and with more success. Madame Ling was reading a novel at home. Mr. Carlyle has quoted Tobias Smollett as to the undesirability of giving the historical muse that latitude which is not uncommon in France; and we prefer to leave the tale of Ling's where Mr. Carlyle left that of Brynhild's wedding.*

* It is a melancholy fact that the Author has quite forgotten what *did* happen! Thus a narrative, probably diverting, is for ever lost, thanks to the modesty of our free Press.

SIEUR DE MONTAIGNE.

The French National Library has recently as it is said, made an acquisition of great value and interest. The books, and better still the notes, of Montaigne, the essayist, have been bought up at the not very exorbitant price of thirty-six thousand francs. The volumes are the beautiful editions of the sixteenth century—the age of great scholars and of printers, like the Estiennes, who were at once men of learning and of taste. It is almost certain that they must be enriched with marginal notes of Montaigne's, and the marginal notes of a great man add even more to the value of a book than the scribblings of circulating library readers detract from its beauty. There is always something characteristic in a man's treatment of his books. Coleridge's marginalia on borrowed works, according to Lamb, were an ornament of value to his friends, if they were lucky enough to get the books back again. Poe's marginalia were of exquisite neatness, though in their printed form they were not very interesting. Thackeray's seem mostly to have taken the shape of slight sketches in illustration of the matter. Scaliger's notes converted a classic into a new and precious edition of one example. Casaubon's, on the other hand, were mere scratches and mnemonic lines and blurs, with which he marked his passage through a book, as roughly as the American woodsman "blazes" his way through a forest. "None could read the comment save himself," and the text was disfigured. We may be sure that Montaigne's marginalia are of a very different value. As he walked up and down in his orchard, or in his library, beneath the rafters engraved with epicurean maxims, he jotted his thoughts hastily on the volume in his hand—on the Pliny, or Suetonius, or Livy. His library was probably not a large one, for he had but a few favourite authors, the Latin historians, moralists, and anecdotists, and for mere amusement Terence and Catullus, Boccaccio and Rabelais. His thoughts fell asleep, he says, if he was not walking about, and his utter want of memory made notes and note-books necessary to him. He who could not remember the names of the most ordinary tools used in agriculture, nor the difference between oats and barley, could never keep in his head his enormous stock of classical anecdotes and modern instances. His thoughts got innocently confused with his recollections, and his note-books will probably show whence he drew many of his stories, and the quotations that remain untraced. They will add also to our knowledge of the man and of his character, though it might seem difficult to give additional traits in the portrait of himself which he has painted with so many minute touches.

With the exception of Dr. Johnson, there is scarcely any great man of letters whom we are enabled to know so intimately as the Sieur de Montaigne. He has told us all about himself; all about his age, as far as it came under his eager and observant eyes; all about the whole world, as far as it made part of his experience. Rousseau is not more frank, and not half so worthy of credit, for Rousseau, like Topsy in the novel, had a taste for "'fessing" offences that he had never committed rather than not "'fess" at all. Montaigne strikes no such attitudes; he does not pose, he does not so much confess as blab. His life stands before the reader "as in a picture." We learn that his childhood was a happier one than usually fell to the lot of children in that age when there was but little honey smeared on the cup of learning. We know that his father taught him Greek in a kind of sport or game, that the same parent's relations with the fair sex were remarkable, and that he had extraordinary strength in his thumb. For his own part, Montaigne was so fresh and full of life that Simon Thomas, a great physician, said it would make a decrepit old man healthy again to live in his company. One thinks of him as a youth like the irrepressible Swiss who amused the *ennui* of Gray.

Even in his old age, Montaigne was a gay, cheerful, untiring traveller, always eager to be going on, delighted with every place he visited, and yet anxious for constant change of scene and for new experience. To be amusingly and simply selfish is ever part of the charm of Montaigne. He adds to his reader's pleasure in life by the keenness with which he relished his own existence, and savoured every little incident as a man relishes the bouquet of wine. Without selfishness, how can this be managed? and without perfect simplicity and the good faith on which he prided himself, how could Montaigne, how could Pepys, have enriched the world as they have done? His essays are among the few works that really and literally make life more opulent with accumulated experience, criticism, reflection, humour. He gives of his rich nature, his lavish exuberance of character, out of that fresh and puissant century to this rather weary one, just as his society in youth might have been given to the sick old man.

Besides what he has to give in this manner, Montaigne seems to express French character, to explain the French genius and the French way of looking at life, more clearly and completely than any other writer. He has at bottom the intense melancholy, the looking forward to the end of all, which is the ground-note of the poetry of Villon, and of Ronsard, as of the prose of Chateaubriand. The panelled library in Montaigne's chateau was carven with mottoes, which were to be charms against too great fear of death. "For my part," he says, "if a man could by any means avoid death, were it by hanging a calf-skin on his limbs, I am one that would not be ashamed of the shift." Happy it is, he thinks, that we do not, as a rule, meet death on a sudden, any more than we encounter the death of youth in one day. But this is only the dark background of the enjoyment of life, to which Montaigne clings, as he says, "even too eagerly." Merely to live, merely to muse over this spectacle of the world, simply to feel, even if the thing felt be agony, and to reflect on the pain, and on how it may best be borne—this is enough for Montaigne. This is his philosophy, reconciling in a way the maxims of the schools that divided the older worlds, the theories of the Stoic and wiser Epicurean. To make each moment yield all that it has of experience, and of reflection on that experience, is his system of existence. Acting on this idea, all contrasts of great and petty, mean and divine, in human nature do not sadden, but delight him. It was part of the play to see the division between the King of Navarre (Henri IV.) and the Duke of Guise. He told Thuanus that he knew the most secret thoughts of both these princes and that he was persuaded that neither of them was of the religion he professed. This scandal gave him no concern, compared with his fear that his own castle would suffer in wars of the League. As to the Reformation, he held it for a hasty, conceited movement on the part of persons who did not know what they were meddling with, and, being a perfect sceptic, he was a perfectly good Churchman. Full of tolerance, good-humour, and content, cheerful in every circumstance, simple and charming, yet melancholy in his hour, Montaigne is a thorough representative of the French spirit in literature. His English translator in 1776 declares that "he meets with a much more favourable entertainment in England than in his native country, a servile nation that has lost all sense of liberty." Like many other notions current in 1776, this theory of Montaigne's popularity at home and abroad has lost its truth. Perhaps it would be more true to say that Montaigne is one of the last authors whom modern taste learns to appreciate. He is a man's author, not a woman's; a tired man's, not a fresh man's. We all come to him, late indeed, but at last, and rest in his panelled library.

THACKERAY'S DRAWINGS.

The advertisements of publishers make a very pleasant sort of reading. They offer, as it were, a distant prospect of the great works of the future, looming in a golden haze of expectation. A gentleman or lady may acquire a reputation for wide research by merely making a careful study of the short paragraphs in the literary papers.

There are three classes of people who take an interest in letters. There are the persons who read books; the much larger class which reads reviews; and, again, they who merely skim over the advertisements of new works. The last set live in a constant enjoyment of the pleasure of expectation; they pretend to themselves that some day they will find time to peruse the volumes in the birth of which they are interested, but, in fact, they live in the future. They are a month ahead of their friends who read reviews, and six months of the students who actually devour books themselves. Not only these eager lovers of literary "shop," but all friends of English humour, must be glad to see that a collection of Mr. Thackeray's sketches and drawings has been prepared for publication.

When the news spread over England of Mr. Thackeray's sudden death, it was felt that a personal loss had been sustained by every one who cared for books and for style. Other men might write themselves out, their invention might become weary; and, indeed, Mr. Thackeray himself felt this fatigue. He wished he could get some one to do "the business" of his stories he told the world in a "Roundabout Paper." The love-making parts of "the business" annoyed him, and made him blush, in the privacy of his study, "as if he were going into an apoplexy." Some signs of this distaste for the work of the novelist were obvious, perhaps, in "Philip," though they did not mar the exquisite tenderness and charm of "Denis Duval." However that might be, his inimitable style was as fresh as ever, with its passages of melancholy, its ease, its flexible strength, and unlooked-for cadences. It was the talk about life, and the tone of that talk, which fell silent when Thackeray died, that we all felt as an irremediable loss. There is an old story that Pindar had never in his lifetime written an ode in praise of Persephone, the goddess of death and the dead, and that after he had departed from among living men, his shade communicated to the priests a new hymn on the Queen of Hades. The works of great writers published after their decease have somewhat of the charm of this fabled hymn; they are voices, familiar and unlooked for, out of the silence. They are even stranger, when they have such a slight and homelike interest as the trifles that fell unheeded from the pen or pencil of one who has done great things in poetry or art. Mr. Thackeray's sketches in the "Orphan of Pimlico" are of this quality —caricatures thrown off to amuse children who are now grown men and women. They have the mark of the old unmistakable style, humorous and sad, and, as last remains, they are to be welcomed and treasured.

Mr. Thackeray's skill with the pencil bore very curious relations to his mastery of the other art, in which lay his strength, but to which perhaps he never gave his love. Everyone has heard how, when a young man, he was anxious to illustrate "Pickwick," which found more fitting artists in Seymour and H. K. Browne. Mr. Thackeray seems to have been well aware of the limitations of his own power as a draughtsman. In one of his "Roundabout Papers" he described the method—the secret so to say—of Rubens; and then goes on to lament the impotence of his own hand, the "pitiful niggling," that cannot reproduce the bold sweep of Ruben's brush.

Thackeray was like Théophile Gautier, who began life as a painter, and who has left to posterity a wonderful etching of his own portrait, pale, romantic, with long sweeping moustache, and hair falling over his shoulders. Both writers found their knowledge of the technique of painting useful in making their appreciation of art and nature more keen and versatile. But Mr. Thackeray's powers had another field—he really did succeed in illustrating some of his own writings. Accomplished his style never was. There was a trace of the old school of caricature in the large noses and thin legs which he gave his figures. Nor was his drawing very correct; the thin legs of the heroes of "The Virginians" are often strangely contorted. He has even placed a thumb on the wrong side of a hand! For all that, he gave to many of his own characters a visible embodiment, which another artist would have missed. Mr. Frederick Walker, for instance, drew Philip Firmin admirably—a large, rough man, with a serious and rather worn face, and a huge blonde beard. Mr. Walker's Philip has probably become the Philip of many readers, but he was not Mr. Thackeray's. It is delightful to be sure, on the other hand, that we have the author's own Captain Costigan before us, in his habit as he lived—the unshaven chin, the battered hat, the high stock, the blue cloak, the whiskeyfied stare, and the swagger. Mr. Thackeray did not do his young men well. Arthur Pendennis is only himself as he sits with Warrington over a morning paper; in his white hat and black band at the Derby, he has not the air of a gentleman. Harry Foker is either a coarse exaggeration, or the modern types of Fokers have improved in demeanour on the great prototype. But Costigan is always perfect; and the nose and wig of

Major Pendennis are ideally correct. In his drawings of women, Mr. Thackeray very much confined himself to two types. There was the dark-eyed, brown-haired, bright-complexioned girl who was his favourite—Laura, Betsinda, Amelia; and the blonde, ringletted, clever, and false girl—Becky, Blanche, Angelica, who was the favourite of the reader. He did not always succeed in making them pretty, though there is a beautiful head of Amelia, in a court dance at Pumpernickel; but he always made the dark young lady look honest, and the fair young minx look a thing all soul and enthusiasm.

It was a note of Mr. Thackeray's art, and probably one among other proofs that the higher fields of art were closed to him, that his success by no means corresponded to the amount of pains he took with his work. His drawings which appeared as steel engravings, were not unfrequently weak, while his sketches on the wood and his lithographs were much more free and masterly. There is, indeed, a sketch on the steel of poor Pen tossing feverishly in his mother's comforting arms, which is full of passion and life and sentiment. But it was rare that success attended his ambition, and, indeed, another drawing of Pen and his mother admiring a sunset might have come out of a book of fashions of that remote period. It was in his initial letters and slight designs that Thackeray showed his best powers. There is much wistful tenderness in the little Marquise's face as she trips down a rope-ladder in an initial letter of *Vanity Fair*. The bewigged shepherds and powdered shepherdesses of his favourite period are always reproduced with grace, and the children of his drawings are almost invariably charming. In the darker moods, when "man delighted him not, nor woman either," children did not fail to please him, and he sketched them in a hundred pathetic attitudes. There are the little brother and sister of the doomed House of Gaunt, sitting under the ancestral sword that seems ready to fall. There is little Rawdon Crawley, manly and stout, in his great coat, watching the thin little cousin Pitt, whom he was "too big a dog to play with." There is the printer's devil, asleep at Pen's door; and the small boy in "Dr. Birch," singing in his nightgown to the big boy in bed. There is Betsinda dancing with her plum-bun in "The Rose and the Ring." The burlesque drawings of that delightful child's book are not its least attraction. Not arriving at the prettiness of Mr. Tenniel, and the elegance of Mr. Du Maurier, and falling far short of their ingenious fantasy, they are yet manly delineations of great adventures. The count kicking the two black men into space is a powerful design, full of action; and it would be hard to beat the picture of the fate of Gruffanuf's husband. These and the rest are old friends, and there are hosts of quaint scribblings, signed with the mark of a pair of spectacles, scattered through the pages of *Punch*.

GOLF.

WHILE pheasant-shooters are enjoying the first day of the season, the votaries of a sport not less noble, though less noisy, are holding the great festival of their year. The autumn meeting of the Royal and Ancient Golf Club of St. Andrews is in full swing, and the words will suggest pleasant memories to many a golfer. Golf is not one of the more brilliant and famous pastimes of the day, though it yields to none in antiquity and in unassuming merit. The names of the winners of the gold medal and of the silver cross are not telegraphed all over the world as widely as Mr. Tennyson's hero wished the news that Maud had accepted him to be. The red man may possibly "dance beneath his red cedar tree" at the tidings of the event of one of our great horse-races, or great university matches. At all events, even if the red man preserves his usual stoicism of demeanour, his neighbours, the pale-faces, like to know all about the result of many English sports the moment they are decided. Golf, as we have said, excites less general enthusiasm; but in people who love it at all, the love is burning, consuming; they will talk golf-shop in season and out of season. Few persons, perhaps, will call golf the very first and queen of games. Cricket exercises more faculties of body, and even of mind, for does not the artful bowler "bowl with his head?" Football demands an extraordinary personal courage, and implies the existence of a fierce delight in battle with one's peers. Tennis, with all its merits, is a game for the few, so rare are tennis-courts and so expensive the pastime. But cricketers, football-players, tennis-players, would all give golf the second place after their favourite exercise; and just as Themistocles was held to be the best Greek general, because each of his fellows placed him second, so golf may assert a right to be thought the first of games. One great advantage it certainly has—it is a game for "men" of all ages, from eight, or even younger, to eighty. The links of St. Andrews are probably cleared just now of the little lads and the veterans; they make room for the heroes, the medalists, the great players—Mr. Mackay, Mr. Lamb, Mr. Leslie Balfour, and the rest. But at ordinary times there are always dozens of tiny boys in knickerbockers and scarlet stockings, who "drive out" the first hole in some twenty strokes of their little clubs, and who pass much of their time in fishing for their lost balls in the muddy burn. As for the veterans "on the threshold of old age," it is pleasant to watch their boyish eagerness, the swaying of their bodies as they watch the short flight of their longest hits; their delight when they do manage to hit further than the sand-pit, or "bunker," which is named after the nose of a long-dead principal of the university; their caution, nay, their almost tedious delay in the process of putting, that is, of hitting the ball over the "green" into the neighbouring hole. They can still do their round, or their two rounds, five or ten miles' walking a day; and who can speak otherwise than well of a game which is not too strenuous for healthy age or tender childhood, and yet allows an athlete of twenty-three to put out all his strength?

Golf is a thoroughly national game; it is as

Scotch as haggis, cockie-leekie, high cheek-bones, or rowanberry jam. A spurious imitation, or an arrested development of the sport, exists in the south of France, where a ball is knocked along the roads to a fixed goal. But this is naturally very poor fun compared to the genuine game as played on the short turf beside the grey northern sea on the coast of Fife. Golf has been introduced of late years into England, and is played at Westward Ho, at Wimbledon, at Blackheath (the oldest club), at Liverpool, over Cowley Marsh, near Oxford, and in many other places. It is, therefore, no longer necessary to say that golf is not a highly developed and scientific sort of hockey, or bandy-ball. Still, there be some to whom the processes of the sport are a mystery, and who would be at a loss to discriminate a niblick from a bunker-iron. The thoroughly equipped golf-player needs an immense variety of weapons, or implements, which are carried for him by his caddie—a youth or old man, who is, as it were, his esquire, who sympathizes with him in defeat, rejoices in his success, and aids him with such advice as his superior knowledge of the ground suggests. The class of human beings known as caddies are the offspring of golf, and have peculiar traits which distinguish them from the professional cricketer, the waterman, the keeper, the gillie, and all other professionals. It is not very easy to account for their little peculiarities. One thing is certain—that when golf was introduced by Scotchmen into France, and found a home at Pau, in the shadow of the Pyrenees, the French caddie sprang, so to speak, from the ground, the perfect likeness of his Scottish brother. He was just as sly, just as importunate in his demands to be employed, just as fond of "putting at short holes," more profane, and every bit as contemptuous of all non-golf-playing humanity as the boyish Scotch caddie, in whom contempt has reversed the usual process, and bred familiarity with all beginners.

The professional cricketer can instruct an unskilled amateur, can take his ill-guarded wicket, and make him "give chances" all over the field, without bursting into yells of unseemly laughter. But the little caddie cannot restrain his joy when the tyro at golf, after missing his ball some six times, ultimately dashes off the head of his club against the ground. Nor is he less exuberant when his patron's ball is deep in a "bunker," or sand-pit, where the wretch stands digging at it with an iron, hot, helpless, and wrathful. And yet golf is a sport not learned in a day, and caddies might be more considerate. The object of the game is to strike a small gutta-percha ball into a hole about five inches wide, distant from the striker about three hundred yards, and separated from him by rough grass and smooth sand-pits, furze bushes, and perhaps a road or a brook. He who, of two players, gets his ball into the hole in the smallest number of strokes is the winner of that hole, and the party then play towards the next hole. All sorts of skill are needed —strength and adroitness, and a certain supple "swing" of the body, are wanted to send the ball "sure and far" in the "driving" part of the game. Nothing is so pleasant as a clean "drive." The sensation is like that of hitting a ball to square-leg, fair and full, at cricket. Then the golfer must have the knack to lift his ball out of deep sand with the "iron," and to strike it deftly "a half-shot" up to the hole with the "cleek;" and, lastly, coolness and a good eye when he "putts" or hits his ball actually up to the very hole.

Any degree of skill in these varied feats makes golf a delightful game, if the opponents are well matched. Nor are the charms of scenery wanting at St. Andrews, the headquarters of the sport. There is no more picturesque town in Scotland than the little university city. From the plain of the estuary of the river Eden, across the long leagues of marsh land and the stretches of golden sand and brown, the towers of St. Andrews—for it is a town of many towers—are seen breaking the sky-line. Built on a windy headland, running out to the grey northern sea, it reaches the water with an ancient pier of rugged stone. Immediately above is the site of a chapel of immemorial age, and above that again are the ruins of the cathedral—gaunt spires with broken tracery, standing where once the burnished roof of copper flashed far across the deep. The high street winds from the cathedral precinct past an old house of Queen Mary Stuart, past ruined chapels of St. Leonard's, and the university chapel with its lovely spire, down to the shores of the bay; and along the bay run the famous "links," where the royal and ancient game has its cradle and home. Other links, as Prestwick, or North Berwick, may vie with those of St. Andrews in extent, or in the smoothness of the putting greens, or in the number and hardness of the "hazards," or difficult places; but none offer so wide and varied an extent of scenery, from the melancholy stretch of the parallel sands to the hills in the west, the golden glitter of the beach, beneath the faint aërial blue of the still more distant hills across the firth, while behind is the city set on its cliffs, and proud with its crown of spires. The reflected sunset lingers on the walls and crags and towers, that shine imaged in the wet sands, the after-glow hangs over the eastern sky, and these have their charm; but their charm yields to that of golf. It is a sign that a man has lost heart and hope when he dilates on the beauty of the scenery, and abstracts his attention from what alone would interest him were he winning—the "lie" of his ball. Who can stop to think of the beauties of nature, when he and his antagonist are equal, and there are only two more holes left to play in the match for the medal? It is a serious moment; not one of the little crowd of observers, the gallery that accompany the players, dares to speak, or even cough. The caddie who sneezes is lost, for he will be accused of distracting his master's attention. The ladies begin to appear in the background, ready to greet the players, and to tell the truth, are not very welcome to the nervous golfer. Everything turns on half an inch of leather in a " drive," or a stiff blade of grass in a putt, and the interest is wound up to a really breathless pitch. Happy he is who does not in his excitement "top" his ball into the neighbouring brook, or "heel" it and send it devious down to the depths of ocean. Happy is he who can "hole out the last hole in four" beneath the eyes of the ladies. Striding victorious into the hospitable club, where beer awaits him, he need not envy the pheasant-slayer who has slain his hundreds.

ART OF DINING.

THERE is such a thing as nationality in dining, just as Mr. Browning has proved, in a brilliant poem, that there is nationality in drinks. Surveying mankind with extensive view, the essayist recognizes that the science is not absolutely ignored in Turkey, where we cannot but think that an archaic school retains too much wool with the mutton, and that dining (like Egyptian Art) is rather a matter of sacred and immemorial rules than in any worthy sense of the word a science. The Chinese and Japanese have long been famous for their birds'-nest soup, and for making the best, after his lamented decease, of the friend of man—the dog. About the Australians and New Zealanders, perhaps the less said the better. Many students will feel that our own colonists have neglected to set a proper example to these poor heathen races, who, save kangaroos, have no larger game than rats. The Englishman in Australia revels in boundless mutton, in damper, in tea, and in the vintages of his adopted soil, which he playfully, and patriotically, compares to those of the Rhine. It is impossible, on the other hand, not to recognize the merits of the Russian *cuisine*, where the imported civilization of France has found various good traditional ideas still retained by the Sclavonic people; and where the *caviare*, "with that pale green hue which denotes the absence of salt," is not to be overlooked. In melancholy contrast to the native genius of the Sclavs is the absolute dearth of taste and sense in gastronomic Germany. If a map of the world could be made—and why not?—in which lands of utter darkness in culinary matters should be coloured black (like heathen countries in the missionary atlas, and coal-fields in the map of physical geography), the German Empire would be one vast blot on Central Europe. Science might track Teutonic blood by the absence of respectable cookery; and in England too obvious tokens would be found of that incapacity of the art of dining which we brought from the marshes of Holstein. In America, nature herself has put the colonists on many schemes for the improvement of dinner, and terrapin soup is gratefully associated with memoirs of Virginia—in the minds of those who like terrapin soup. The canvas-backed duck has been praised as highly as the "swopping, swopping mallard" of a comfortable college in Oxford. As to the wild turkey, the poet has not yet risen in America who can do justice to the charms of that admirable bird. Mr. Whitman, who has much to say about "bob-a-links" and "whip-poor-wills," and some other fowl which sing "when lilacs bloom in the garden yard," has neglected, we fear the wild turkey, simply because the Muse has not given this bird melody, and made it, like the robin-redbreast, which goes so well with bread-crumbs, "an amiable songster." American genius neglects the turkey, and positively takes more interest in the migrations of the transatlantic sparrow. If the nobler fowl can cross the water as safely as the beef and mutton of everyday life, he will receive the honour he deserves in this country. Some students with the deathless thirst of scientific men for acclimatization, speak well of the

Bohemian pheasant, which, unlike some other denizens of Bohemia, is fat. But there are probably less familiar birds in America that rival the duck and the wild turkey, and excel the Bohemian pheasant. The existence of maize, however, on the Western Continent has been a snare to American cooks, who have yielded to an absorbing passion for hot corn-cakes.

France is, of course, the land in which the Muse of cooking is native. "If we turn north towards Belgium," says a modern author, "we shall find much that is good in cooking and eating known, if not universally practised." He has also made the discovery that the Belgian air and climate are admirably suited to develop the best qualities of Burgundy. It is from these favoured and ingenious people that England ought to learn a lesson, or rather a good many lessons. To begin at the beginning, with soup, does not every one know that all domestic soups in England, which bear French names, are really the same soup, just as almost all puddings are, or may be, called cabinet pudding? The one word "Julienne" covers all the watery, chill and tasteless, or terribly salt, decoctions, in which

F

a few shreds of vegetables appear drifting through the illimitable inane. Other names are given at will by the help of a cookery-book and a French dictionary; but all these soups, at bottom, are attempts to be Julienne soup. The idea of looking on soup "as a vehicle for applying to the palate certain herbal flavours," is remote indeed from the Plain Cook's mind. There is a deeply rooted conviction in her inmost soul that all vegetables, which are not potatoes or cabbages, partake of the nature of evil. As to eating vegetables apart from meat, it was once as hard to get English domestics to let you do that, as to get a Cretan cook to serve woodcock with the trail. "*Kopros* is not a thing to be eaten," says the Cretan, according to a traveller; and the natural heart of the English race regards vegetables, when eaten as a *plat* apart, with equal disfavour. Probably the market gardener's ignorance and conservatism are partly in fault. Cabbage he knows, and potatoes he knows, but what are pennyroyal and chervil? He has cauliflower for you, but never says, "Here is rue for you, and rosemary for you." Cooks do not give him botany lessons, and a Scottish cook, deprived of bay-leaf, has been known to make an experiment in the use of what she called "Roderick Randoms," members of the vegetable kingdom which proved to be rhododendron. As for pennyroyal, most people have only heard of it through Mr. Bohn's crib to Aristophanes.

When it comes to fish, it is allowed that we are not an insular people for nothing. There are other forms of good living that Paris knows not of, so to speak, at first hand, native to England. Turtle soup, turbot and lobster sauce, a haunch of venison, and a grouse, are, we may say without chauvinism, a "truly royal repast." But we incur the contempt of foreigners once more in the matter of wines. To like sherry, the coarse and fiery, is a matter of habit, which would teach us to love betel-root, and rejoice in the very peculiar drink of the South Sea islanders. Some purists include champagne in the same condemnation—the champagne, that is, of this degenerate day. When the Russians drank up the contents of the widow Clicquot's cellars, they found a sweet natural wine, to which they have constantly adhered. But Western Europe, all the Europe which, as M. Comte puts it, "synergizes" after light and positivism, has tended towards champagnes more or less dry. The English serve this "grog mousseux" as a necessity for social liveliness, and have not come back to the sweet wine which was only meant to be drunk with sweets. A *Quarterly* reviewer is very severe in his condemnation of a practice which will only yield to the stress of some European convulsion in politics and society. These matters are like certain large reforms, they either come to pass without observation in the slow changes of things, or great movements in the world are accompanied by small ones in everyday life. Dry champagne came in after the Revolution; it may go out after a European war, which will make wine either expensive, or, if cheap, a palpably spurious article. "Monotony and base servile imitation" may be the bane of eating and drinking in England; but the existence of monotony shows that the English really do not care very much about dining considered as a fine art. When they do care, they cover their interest in the matter decently, with the veil of humorous affectation. They cannot spontaneously and sincerely make a business of it, as the French do in all good faith. Even if they had a genius for dining, we doubt if a critic is right in thinking they should dine at six o'clock or seven at latest. Whether in the country or in town, the business or amusement of the day claims more time. Sportsmen, for example, in early autumn could not possibly return home by six very frequently; and in summer six o'clock may be so sultry an hour that the thought of food is intolerable. Still, it must be admitted that the unawakened state of the market-gardener and the condition of English soups are matters deserving serious consideration.

AMERICAN HUMOUR.

ONE of the most popular of American humorists has elicited from a member of an English audience, who did not quite hear him lecture, a remark of an amusing sort. The aggrieved listener proclaimed that he "had a right to hear." This was one of the turbulent people who should read Mazzini, and learn that man has no rights worth mentioning—only duties, one of which is to hold his tongue in season. If Mr. Bret Harte's words did not reach all his audience, his writings at least have come home to most English readers. They suggest a consideration of the many points of difference which distinguish American from English humour. The Americans are of our own stock, yet in their treatment of the ludicrous how unlike us they are! As far as fun goes, the race has certainly become "differentiated," as the philosophers say, on the other side of the Atlantic. It does not seem probable that the infusion of alien blood has caused the difference. The native redskin can claim few descendants among the civilized Americans, and the native redskin had no sense of humour. We all remember Cooper's Hawkeye or Leather Stocking, with his "peculiar silent laugh." He was obliged to laugh silently for fear of attracting the unfavourable notice of the Mingo, who might be hiding in the nearest bush. The red men found it simpler and safer not to laugh at all. No, it is not from the natives that the people of the States get their peculiar fun. As to the German emigrants—— But why pursue the subject? The Abbé Bouhours told the bitter truth about German wit, though, in new conditions and on a fresh soil, the Teuton has helped to produce Hans Breitmann. We laugh at Hans, however, and with his creator. Hans does not make us laugh by conscious efforts of humour. Whence, then, come Artemus Ward, Mark Twain, and Mr. Bret Harte, who are probably the American humorists whose popularity is widest? Mr. Bret Harte's own fun is much more English and less thoroughly Yankee than that of his contemporaries. He is a disciple of Thackeray and Dickens. Of all the pupils of Dickens he is perhaps the only one who has continued to be himself, who has not fallen into a trick of aping his master's mannerisms. His mixture of the serious, the earnest, the pathetic, makes his humour not unlike the melancholy mirth of Thackeray and Sterne. He is almost the only American humorist with sentiment. It is only the air, not the spirit, that is changed — *cælum non animus*.

The changed atmosphere, the new conditions, do, however, make an immense superficial difference between the humour even of Mr. Bret Harte and that of English writers. His fun is derived from the vagaries of huge, rough people, with the comic cruelty of the old Danes, and with the unexpected tenderness of a sentimental time. The characters of the great Texan and Californian drama are like our hackneyed friends, the Vikings, with a touch, if we may use the term, of spooniness. Their humour is often nothing more than a disdainful trifling with death; they seize the comic side of manslaughter very promptly, and enjoy all the mirth that can be got out of revolvers and grizzly bears.

In Mr. Bret Harte's poems of "The Spelling Bee" and of "The Break-up of the Society upon the Stanislaw," the fun is of this practical sort. The innate mirthfulness of a chunk of old red sandstone is illustrated, and you are introduced to people who not only take delight of battle with their peers, but think the said battle the most killing joke in the world. The incongruities of these revels of wild men in a new world; their confusion when civilization meets them in the shape of a respectable woman or of a baby; their grotesque way of clinging to religion, as they understand it, make up the transatlantic element in this American humour. The rest of it is "European quite," though none the worse for that. It is more humane, on the whole, than the laughable and amazing paradoxes of Mark Twain, or the *naïvetés* of Artemus Ward.

Two remarkable features in American humour, as it is shown in the great body of comic writers who are represented by Mark Twain and the "Genial Showman," are its rusticity and its puritanism. The fun is the fun of rough villagers, who use quaint, straightforward words, and have developed, or carried over in the *Mayflower*, a slang of their own. They do not want anything too refined; they are not in the least like the farm-lad to whose shirt a serpent clung as he was dressing after bathing. Many people have read how he fled into the farm-yard, where the maidens were busy; how he did not dare to stop, and sought escape, not from woman's help—he was too modest—but in running so fast that, obedient to the laws of centrifugal motion, the snake waved out behind him like a flag. The village wits are not so shy. The young ladies, like Betsy Ward, say, "If you mean getting hitched, I'm on." The public is not above the most practical jokes, and a good deal of the amusement is derived from the extreme dryness, the countrified slowness of the narrative. The humorists are Puritans at bottom, as well as rustics. They have an amazing familiarity with certain religious ideas and certain Biblical terms. There is a kind of audacity in their use of the Scriptures, which reminds one of the freedom of mediæval mystery-plays. Probably this boldness began not in scepticism or in irreverence, but in honest familiar faith. It certainly seems very odd to us in England, and probably expressions often get a laugh which would pass unnoticed in America. An astounding coolness and freedom of manners probably go for something in the effect produced by American humour. There is nothing of the social flunkeyism in it which too often marks our own satirists. Artemus Ward's reports of his own conversations with the mighty of the earth were made highly ludicrous by the homely want of self-consciousness, displayed by the owner of the Kangaroo, that "amoosin' little cuss," and of the "two moral B'ars." But it is vain to attempt to analyze the fun of Artemus Ward. Why did he make some people laugh till they cried, while others were all untouched? His secret probably was almost entirely one of manner, a trick of almost idiotic *naïveté*, like that of Lord Dundreary, covering real shrewdness. He had his rustic chaff, his Puritan profanity; his manner was the essence of his mirth. It was one of the ultimate constituents of the ludicrous, beyond which it is useless to inquire.

With Mark Twain we are on smoother ground. An almost Mephistophilean coolness, an unwearying search after the comic sides of serious subjects, after the mean possibilities of the sublime,—these, with a native sense of incongruities and a glorious vein of exaggeration, make up his stock-in-trade. The colossal exaggeration is, of course, natural to a land of ocean-like rivers and almighty tall pumpkins. No one has made such charming use of the trick as Mark Twain. The dryness of the story of a greenhorn's sufferings who had purchased "a genuine Mexican plug," is one of the funniest things in literature. The intense gravity and self-pity of the sufferer, the enormous and Gargantuan feats of his steed, the extreme distress of body thence resulting, make up a passage more moving than anything in Rabelais. The same contrast, between an innocent style of narrative and the huge palpable nonsense of the story told, marks the tale of the agricultural newspaper which Mr. Twain edited. To a joker of jokes of this sort, a tour through Palestine presented irresistible attractions. It is when we read of the "Innocents Abroad" that we discern the weak point of American humour when carried to its extreme. Here, indeed, is the place where the most peculiarly American fun has always failed. It has lacked reverence and sympathy, and so, when it was most itself, never approached the masterpieces of Thackeray and Dickens. To balance its defect by its merit, American humour has always dared to speak out, and Mark Twain especially has hit hard the errors of public opinion and the dishonest compromises of custom.

SUSPENDED ANIMATION.

It used to be thought that a man who said he liked dry champagne would say anything. In the same way, some persons may hold that a person who could believe in the recurrent Australian story of "suspended animation"—artificially produced in animals, and prolonged for months—could believe in anything. It does not do, however, to be too dogmatic about matters of opinion in this world. Perhaps the Australian tale of an invention by which sheep and oxen are first made lifeless, then rendered "stiff ones" by freezing, and then restored to life, and reproduced with gravy, may be like the genius of Beethoven. Very few persons (and these artists) believed in Beethoven at first, but now he is often considered to be the greatest of composers. Perhaps great discoveries, like the works of men of original genius, are certain to be received at first with incredulity and mockery. We will not, therefore, take up a dogmatic position, either about the painting or the preserved meats of the future ; but will hope for the best. The ideally best, of course, is that the tale from Australia may prove true. In that case the poorest will be able to earn "three square meals a day," like the Australians themselves ; and while English butchers suffer (for some one must suffer in all great revolutions), smiling Plenty will walk through our land studying a cookery-book. There are optimistic thinkers, who gravely argue that the serious desires of humanity are the pledges of their own future fulfilment. If that be correct, the Australian myth may be founded on fact. There is no desire more deep-rooted in our perishable nature than that which asks for plenty of beef and mutton at low prices. Again, humanity has so often turned over the idea of conveniently suspended animation before, that there must be something in that conception. If we examine the history of ideas we shall find that they at first exist "in the air." They float about, beautiful alluring visions, ready to be caught and made to serve mortal needs by the right man at the right moment. Thus Empedocles, Lucretius, and the author of "Vestiges of Creation," all found out Darwinism before Mr. Darwin. They spied the idea, but they left it floating; they did not trap it, and break it into scientific harness. Solomon De Caus, as all the world has heard, was put into a lunatic asylum for inventing the steam-engine, though no one would have doubted his sanity if he had offered to raise the devil, or to produce the philosopher's stone, or the *elixir vitæ*. Now, these precious possessions have not been more in men's minds than a system of conveniently suspended animation. There is scarcely a peasantry in Europe that does not sing the ballad of the dead bride. This lady, in the legends, always loves the cavalier not selected by her parents, the detrimental cavalier. To avoid the wedding which is thrust on her, she gets an old witch to do what the Australian romancer professes to do—to suspend her animation, and so she is carried on an open bier to a chapel on the border of her lover's lands. There he rides, the right lover, with his men-at-arms; the bride revives just in time, is lifted on to his saddle-bow, and "they need swift steeds that follow" the fugitive pair. The sleeping beauty, who is thrown into so long a swoon by the prick of the fairy thorn, is another very old example; while "Snow-white," in her glass coffin, in the German nursery tale, is a third instance.

It is not only the early fancy of the ballad-mongers and fairy tale-tellers that has dwelt longingly on the idea of suspended animation. All the mystics, who all follow the same dim track that leads to nothing, have believed in various forms of the imaginary Australian experiment. The seers of most tribes, from Kamschatka to Zululand, and thence to Australia, are feigned to be able to send their souls away, while their bodies lie passive in the magical tent. The soul wanders over the earthly world, and even to the home of the dead, and returns, in the shape of a butterfly or of a serpent, to the body which has been lying motionless, but uncorruptible, in apparent death. The Indian Yogis can attain that third state of being, all three being unknown to Brahma, which is neither sleeping nor waking, but trance. To produce this ecstasy, to do for themselves what some people at the Antipodes pretend to do to sheep and cattle, is the ideal aim of the existence of the Yogi. The Neoplatonists were no wiser, and Greek legend tells a well-known story of a married mystic whose suspended animation began at last to bore his wife "Dear Hermotimus"—that was his name, if we have not forgotten it—"is quite the most absent of men," his spouse would say, when her husband's soul left his body and took its walks abroad. On one occasion the philosopher's spiritual part remained abroad so long that his lady ceased to expect its return. She therefore went through the usual mourning, cut her hair, cried, and finally burned the body on the funeral-pyre. "We can do no more for miserable mortals, when once the spirit has left their bones," says Homer.

At that very moment the spirit returned, and found its uninsured tenement of clay reduced to ashes. The sequel may be found in a poem of the late Professor Aytoun's, and in the same volume occurs the wondrous tale of Colonel Townsend, who could suspend his animation at pleasure.

There is certainly a good deal of risk, as well as of convenience, in suspended animation. People do not always welcome Rip Van Winkle when he returns to life, as we would all welcome Mr. Jefferson if he revisited the glimpses of the footlights.

> "The hard heir strides about the lands,
> And will not yield them for a day."

There is the horrible chance of being buried alive, which was always present to the mind of Edgar Poe. It occurs in one of his half-humorous stories, where a cataleptic man, suddenly waking in a narrow bed, in the smell of earthy mould, believes he has been interred, but finds himself mistaken. In the "Fall of The House of Usher" the wretched brother, with his nervous intensity of sensation, hears his sister for four days stirring in her vault before she makes her escape. In the "Strange Effects of Mesmerism on a Dying Man," the animation is mesmerically suspended at the very instant when it was about naturally to cease. The results, when the passes were reversed, and the half fled life was half restored, are described in a passage not to be recommended to sensitive readers. M. About, uses the same general idea in the fantastic plot of his "L'Homme à l'Oreille Cassée," and the risk of breakage was insisted on by M. About as well as by the inventive Australian reporter. Mr. Clarke Russell has also frozen a Pirate. Thus the idea of suspended animation is "in the air," is floating among the visions of men of genius. It is, perhaps, for the great continent beneath the Southern Cross to realize the dreams of savages, of seers, of novelists, of poets, of Yogis, of Plotinus, of M. About, and of Swedenborg. Swedenborg, too, was a suspended animationist, if we may use the term. What else than suspension of outer life was his "internal breathing," by which his body existed while his soul was in heaven, hell, or the ends of the earth? When the Australian discovery is universally believed in (and acted on), then, and perhaps not till then, will be the time for the great unappreciated. They will go quietly to sleep, to waken a hundred years hence, and learn how posterity likes their pictures and poems. They may not always be satisfied with the results; but no artist will disbelieve in the favourable verdict of posterity till the supposed Australian method is applied to men as well as to sheep and kangaroos.

BREAKING UP.

THE schools have by this time all "broken up," if that is still the term which expresses the beginning of their vacation. "Breaking up" is no longer the festival that it was in the good old coaching days—nothing is what it was in the good old coaching days. Boys can no longer pass a whole happy day driving through the country and firing peas at the wayfaring man. They have to travel by railway, and other voyagers may well pray that their flight be not on breaking-up day. The untrammeled spirits of boyhood are very much what they have always been. Boys fill the carriages to overflowing. They sing, they shout, they devour extraordinary quantities of refreshment, they buy whole libraries of railway novels, and, generally speaking, behave as if the earth and the fulness of it were their own. This is trying to the mature traveller, who has plenty of luggage on his mind, and who wishes to sleep or to read the newspaper. Boys have an extraordinary knack of losing their own luggage, and of appearing at home, like the companions of Ulysses, "bearing with them only empty hands." This is usually their first exploit in the holidays. Their arrival causes great excitement among their little sisters, and in the breasts of their fathers wakens a presentiment of woe. When a little boy comes home his first idea is to indulge in harmless swagger. When Tom Tulliver went to school, he took some percussion caps with him that the other lads might suppose him to be familiar with the use of guns. The schoolboy has other devices for keeping up the manly character in the family circle. The younger ones gather round him while he narrates the adventures of himself, and Smith minor, and Walker (of Briggs's house), in a truly epic spirit. He has made unheard-of expeditions up the river, has chaffed a farmer almost into apoplexy, has come in fifth in the house paper-chase, has put the French master to open shame, and has got his twenty-two colours. These are the things that make a boy respected by his younger brothers, and admired by his still younger sisters. They of course have a good deal to tell him. The setter puppies must be inspected. A match is being got up with the village eleven, who are boastful and confident in the possession of a bowling curate. To this the family hero rejoins that "he will crump the parson," a threat not so awful as it sounds. There is a wasps' nest which has been carefully preserved for this eventful hour, and which is to be besieged with boiling water, gunpowder, and other engines of warfare. Thus the schoolboy's first days at home are a glorious hour of crowded sport.

It cannot be denied that, as the holidays go on, a biggish boy sometimes finds time hang heavy on his hands, while his father and mother find him hang heavy on theirs. The first excitement rubs off. The fun of getting up handicap races among children under twelve years of age wears away. One cannot always be taking wasps' nests. Of course there are many happy boys who live in the country, and pursue the pleasures of manhood with the zest of extreme youth. Before they are fourteen, they have a rod on a salmon river, a gun on a moor, horses and

yachts, and boats at their will, with keepers
and gillies to do their bidding. Others, not
so much indulged by fortune and fond
parents, live at least among hills and streams,
or by the sea. They are never "in the way,"
for they are always in the open air. Their
summer holidays may be things to look back
upon all through life. Natural history, and
the beauty of solitary nature; the joys of the
swimmer in deep river pools shut in with cool
grey walls of rock, and fringed with fern; the
loveliness of the high table lands, and the
intense hush that follows sunset by the trout
stream—these things are theirs, and become
a part of their consciousness. In later and
wearier years these spectacles will flash before
their eyes unbidden, they will see the water
dimpled by rising trout, and watch the cattle
stealing through the ford, and disappearing,
grey shapes, in the grey of the hills.

In boyhood, the legends that cling to
ancient castles where only a shell of stone
is standing, and to the ash-trees that grow by
the feudal gateway, and supplied the wood
for spear shafts—these and all the stories of
red men that haunt the moors, and of kelpies
that make their dwelling in the waters, become

very real to us when standing in the dusk by a moorland loch. If some otter or great fish breaks the water and the stillness with a sudden splash, a boy feels a romantic thrill, a pause of expectation, that later he will never experience. "The thoughts of a boy are long, long thoughts," says the poet; he thinks them out by himself on the downs, or the hills, and tells them to nobody.

If we all lived in the country, the advent of boys would not be a thing to contemplate with secret dread. It is rather a terrible thing, a houseful of boys in a town, or in a pretty thickly populated district. Boys, it is true, are always a source of pleasure to the humorist and the scientific observer of mankind. They are scarcely our fellow-creatures, so to speak; they live in a world of their own, ruled by eccentric traditional laws. They have their own heroes, and are much more interested in Mr. Alan Steel or Lohmann than in persons like Mr. Arthur Balfour, whose cricket is only middling. They have rules of conduct which cannot be called immoral, but which are certainly relics of a very ancient state of tribal morality. The humour of it is that the modern boy is so grave, so self-assured, and has such abundance of aplomb. He has acquired an air of mysterious sagacity, and occasionally seems to smile at the petty interests with which men divert themselves. In a suburban or city home, he can find very little that he thinks worth doing, and then he becomes discontented and disagreeable. It is better that he should do that, perhaps, than that he should aim at being a dandy. The boy-dandy is an odd, and at bottom a slovenly, creature. He is fond of varnished boots, of pink neckties, of lavender-coloured gloves and, above all, of scent. The quantity of scent that a lad of sixteen will pour on his handkerchief is something perfectly astounding. In this stage of his development he is addicted to falling into love, or rather into flirtation. He keeps up a correspondence with a young lady in Miss Pinkerton's establishment. They see each other in church, when he looks unutterable things from the gallery. This kind of boy is not unlikely to interest himself, speculatively, in horse-races. He has communications with a bookmaker who finds Boulogne a salubrious residence. He would like to know the officers, if his home is in a garrison town, and he humbly imitates these warriors at an immense distance. He passes much time in trying to colour a pipe. This is not a nice sort of boy to have at home for the holidays, nor is it likely that he does much good when he is at school. It is pleasanter to think of the countless jolly little fellows of twelve, who are happily busy all day with lawn-tennis, cricket, and general diversion in the open air. Their appearance, their manly frankness, their modesty and good temper, make their homes happier in the holidays than in the quieter nine months of the year. Let us hope that they will not put off their holiday tasks to be learned in the train on their way back to school. This, alas, is the manner of boyhood.

ON SHAVING.

A PHILANTHROPIST has published a little book which interests persons who in civilized society form a respectable minority, and in the savage world an overpowering majority. But, savage or polite, almost all men must shave, or must be shaved; and the author of "A Few Useful Hints on Shaving," is, in his degree, a benefactor to his fellow-creatures. The mere existence of the beard may be accounted for in various ways; but, however we explain it, the beard is apt to prove a nuisance to its proprietor. Speculators of the old school may explain the beard as part of the punishment entailed on man with the curse of labour. The toilsome day begins with the task of scraping the chin and contemplating, as the process goes on, a face that day by day grows older and more weary. No race that shaves can shirk the sense of passing time, or be unaware of the approach of wrinkles, of "crow's-feet," of greyness. Shaving is the most melancholy, and to many people the most laborious of labours. It seems, therefore, more plausible (if less scientific) to look on the beard as a penalty for some ancient offence of our race, than to say with Mr. Grant Allen, and perhaps other disciples of Mr. Darwin, that the beard is the survival of a very primitive decoration. According to this view man was originally very hairy. His hair wore off in patches as he acquired the habits of sleeping on his sides and of sitting with his back against a tree, or against the wall of his hut. The hair of dogs is not worn off thus, but what of that? After some hundreds of thousands of years had passed, our ancestors (according to this system) awoke to the consciousness that they were patchy and spotty, and they determined to eradicate all hair that was not ornamental. The eyebrows, moustache, and, unfortunately, the beard seemed to most races worth preserving. There are, indeed, some happy peoples who have no beards, or none worth notice. Very early in their history they must have taken the great resolve to "live down" and root out the martial growth that fringes our lips. But among European peoples the absence of a beard has usually been a reproach, and the enemies of Njal, in ancient Iceland, could find nothing worse to say of him than that he was beardless. Mehemet Ali bought sham beards for his Egyptian grenadiers, that they might more closely resemble the European model. The soldiers of Harold thought that the Normans were all priests, because they were "shavelings;" and it is only natural that soldiers should in all countries be bearded. It is almost impossible to shave during a campaign. Stendhal, the French novelist and critic, was remarkable as the best, perhaps the only, clean-shaved man in the French army during the dreadful retreat from Moscow. In his time, as in that of our fathers, ideas of beauty had changed, and the smooth chin was as much the mark of a gentleman as the bearded chin had been the token of a man.

The idea that shaving is a duty—ceremonial, as among the Egyptian priests, or social merely, as among ourselves—is older than the invention of steel or even of bronze razors. Nothing is more remarkable in savage life than the resolution of the braves who shave with a shell or with a broken piece of glass, left by European mariners. A warrior will throw himself upon the ground, and while one friend sits on his head, and another holds his arms and prevents him from struggling, a third will scrape his chin with the shell or the broken bottle-glass till he rises, bleeding, but beardless. Macaulay, it seems, must have shaved almost as badly with the razor of modern life. When he went to a barber, and, after an easy shave, asked what he owed, the fellow replied, "Just what you generally give the man who shaves you, sir." "I generally give him two cuts on each cheek," said the historian of England. Shaving requires a combination of qualities which rarely meet in one amateur. You should have plenty of razors, unlike a Prussian ambassador of the stingy Frederick. This ambassador, according to Voltaire, cut his throat with the only razor he possessed. The chin of that diplomatist must have been unworthy alike of the Court to which he was accredited, and of that from which he came. The exquisite shaver who would face the world with a smooth chin requires many razors, many strops, many brushes, odd soaps, a light steady hand, and, perhaps, a certain gaiety of temper which prevents edged weapons from offering unholy temptations. Possibly the shaver is born, not made, like the poet; it is sure that many men are born with an inability to shave. Hence comes the need for the kindly race of barbers, a race dear to literature. Their shops were the earliest clubs, their conversation was all the ancient world knew in the way of society journals. Horace, George Eliot, Beaumarchais, Cervantes, and Scott have appreciated the barber, and celebrated his characteristics. If the wearing of the beard ever became universal, the world, and especially the Spanish and Italian world, would sadly miss the barber and the barber's shop. The energy of the British character our zeal for individual enterprise, makes us a self-shaving race; the Latin peoples are economical, but they do not grudge paying for an easy shave. Americans in this matter are more Continental than English in their taste. Was it not in Marseilles that his friends induced Mark Twain to be shaved by a barber worthy of the bottle-glass or seashell stage of his profession? They pretended that his performances were equal to those of the barber on board the ship that brought them from America.

Englishmen, as a rule, shave themselves when they do not wear beards. The author of the little pamphlet before us gives a dozen curious hints which prove the difficulty of the art. Almost all razors, he seems to think, were "made to sell." He suggests that razors of tried and trusty character, razors whose public form can be depended upon, should be purchased of barbers. But it is not every barber who will part with such possessions. Razors are like Scotch sheep dogs; no one would keep a bad one, or sell, or give away a good one. Cœlebs did not find the quest of a wife more arduous than all men find that of a really responsible razor. You may be unlucky in the important matter of lather. For soap our author gives a recipe which reminds one of Walton's quaint prescriptions and queer preparations. Shaving soap should be made at home, it seems, and the mystery of its manufacture is here disclosed. The only way to keep razors "set" is to persevere in sending them to various barbers till the genius who can "set" them to your hand is discovered. Perhaps he lives at Aleppo;

perhaps, like the father of a heroine of comic song, at Jerusalem. Till he is discovered the shaver wins no secure happiness, and in the search for the barber who has an elective affinity for the shaver may be found material for an operetta or an epic. The shaver figures as a sort of Alastor, seeking the ideal setter of razors, as Shelley's Alastor sought ideal beauty in the neighbourhood of Afghanistan, and in the very home of the Central Asian Question. No razor should be condemned till it has been "stropped" well and carefully. And this brings us to the great topic of strops. Some say that soldiers' old buff belts make the best strops. The Scotch peasantry use a peculiar hard smooth fungus which grows in decaying elm trees. Our author has heard that "Government now demands the return of" the old buff belts. Government cannot want them all for its own use, and perhaps will see to it that old buff strops once more find an open market. In the lack of old buff belts, you may mix up tallow and the ashes of burnt newspaper, and smear this unctuous compound on the strop. People who neglect these "tips," and who are clumsy, like most of us, may waste a forty-eighth part of their adult years in shaving. This time is worth economizing, and with a little forethought, an ideal razor-setter, tallow, buff belts, burnt newspapers, and the rest, we may shave in five minutes daily.

STREET NOISES.

"If any calm, a calm despair," is the portion of people who would like to reform, that is to abolish, the street noises of London. These noises are constantly commented upon with much freedom in the columns of various contemporaries. Nor is this remarkable, for persons who are occupied with what is called "brainwork," are peculiarly sensitive to the disturbances of the streets. Sometimes they cannot sleep till morning, sometimes they can only sleep in the earlier watches of the night, and, as a rule, they cannot write novels, or articles, or treatises; they cannot compose comic operas, or paint, in the midst of a row. Now, the streets of London are the scenes of rows at every hour of night and day-light. It is not the roll of carriages and carts that provokes irritation, and drives the sensitive man or woman half mad. Even the whistling of the metropolitan trains may, perhaps, be borne with if the drivers are not too ambitious artists, and do not attempt fantasias and variations on their powerful instrument. The noises that ruin health, temper, and power of work; the noises that cause an incalculable waste of time, money, and power, are all voluntary, and perhaps preventable. Let us examine the working hours of the nervous or irritable musician, mathematician, man of letters, or member of Parliament. On second thoughts, the last may be omitted, as if he cannot sleep in a tedious debate, his case is beyond cure.

> "Not bromide of potassium
> Nor all the drowsy speeches in the world"

can medicine him to forgetfulness of street noises. For the others, the day may be said to begin about five, when the voice of the chimney-sweep is heard in the land. Here we may observe that servants are the real causes of half the most provoking noises in London. People ask why the sweep cannot ring the bell, like other people. But the same people remark that even the howl of the sweep does not waken the neighbours' servants. Of what avail, then, could his use of the bell prove? It generally takes the sweep twenty-five minutes exactly to bring the servants to open the door. Meanwhile, the eminent men of letters in the street open their windows, and show a very fair command of language understanded by the people. But the sweep only laughs, and every three minutes utters a howl which resembles no other noise with which men are acquainted. Where do young sweeps learn to make this cry which can only be acquired by long practice? Perhaps it is inherited, like the music of "the damned nightingales," as the sleepless political economist called the Daulian birds.

When the sweep is silent, when slumber is stealing over the weary eyelids, then traction engines, or steam-rollers, or some other scientific improvement on wheels begin to traverse the streets and shake the houses. This does not last more than a quarter of an hour, and then a big bell rings, and the working men and women tramp gaily by, chatting noisily and in excellent spirits. Now comes the milkman's turn. He, like the chimney-sweep, has his own howl, softer, more flute-like in quality than that of the sweep, but still capable of waking any one who is not a domestic servant in hard training. The milkman also cries "woa" to his horse at every house, and accompanies himself on his great tin cans, making a noise most tolerable, and not to be endured. Is it necessary, absolutely necessary, that the milkman should howl? In some parts of town milkwomen distribute their wares without howling. They do, certainly, wear very short petticoats, but that is matter, as Aristotle says, for a separate disquisition. On the other hand, milkwomen exist who howl as loudly as milkmen. We cannot but fear that without these noises it would be difficult to attract the notice of servants. If this pessimistic view be correct, sweeps and milkmen will howl while London is a city inhabited. And even if we could secure the services of milkwomen of the silent species that ring the bell, could we hope to have female chimney-sweeps as well behaved? Here, at all events, is a new opening for female labour. When the milkman has done his worst, the watercress people come and mournfully ejaculate. Now it is time for the sleepless and nervous to get up and do their work. Now, too, the barrel-organ comes round. There are persons who, fortunately for themselves, are so indifferent to music that they do not mind the barrel-organ. It is neither better nor worse to them than the notes of Patti, and from the voice of that siren, as from all music, they withdraw their attention without difficulty. But other persons cannot work while the dirty grinder and the women that drag his instrument are within hearing. The barrel-organ, again, is strong in the support of servants, especially nurses, who find that the music diverts babies. The rest of the day is made hideous by the awful notes of every species of unintelligible and uncalled for costermonger, from him who (apparently) bellows "Annie Erskine," to her who cries, "All a-blowing and a-growing." There are miscreants who want to buy bones, to sell ferns, to sell images, wicker-chairs, and other inutilities, while last come the two men who howl in a discordant chorus, and attempt to dispose of the second edition of the evening paper, at ten o'clock at night. At eleven all the neighbours turn out their dogs to bark, and the dogs waken the cats, which scream like demoniacs. Then the public houses close, and the people who have been inebriated, if not cheered, stagger howling by. Stragglers yell and swear, and use foul language till about four in the morning, without attracting the unfavourable notice of the police. Two or three half drunken men and women bellow and blaspheme opposite the sufferer's house for an hour at a time. And then the chimney-sweep renews his rounds, and the milkman follows him.

The screams of costermongers and of rowdies might surely be suppressed by the police. A system of " local option " might be introduced. In all decent quarters householders would vote against the licensed bellowings of cads and costermongers. In districts which think a noise pleasant and lively the voting would go the other way. People would know where they could be quiet, and where noise would reign. Except Bologna, perhaps no town is so noisy as London; but then, compared with Bologna, London is tranquillity itself. It is fair to say that really nervous and irritable people find the country worse than town. The noise of the nightingales is deplorable. The lamentations of a cow deprived of her calf, or of a passion-stricken cow, " wailing for her demon lover" on the next farm, excel anything that the milkman can perpetrate, and almost vie with the performances of the sweep. When "the cocks are crowing a merry midnight," as in the ballad, the sleepless patient wishes he could make off as quietly and quickly as the ghostly sons of the "Wife of Usher's Well." Dogs delight to bark in the country more than in town. Leech's picture of the unfortunate victim who left London to avoid noise, and found that the country was haunted by Cochin-China cocks, illustrates the still repose of the rural life. Nervous people, on the whole, are in a minute minority. No one else seems to mind how loud and horrible the noises of London are, and therefore we have faint hope of seeing nocturnal 'Arry gagged, the drunken drab "moved on," and the sweep compelled to ring the bell till some one comes and opens the door of the house in whose chimneys he is professionally interested.

LENDING OF BOOKS.

A POPULAR clergyman has found it necessary to appeal to his friends in a very touching way. The friends of the divine are requested to return "Colenso on the Pentateuch," and another volume which they have borrowed. The advertisement has none of that irony which finds play in the notice, "The Gentleman who took a brown silk umbrella, with gold crutch handle, and left a blue cotton article, is asked to restore the former." The advertiser seems to speak more in sorrow and in hope than in anger, and we sincerely trust that he may get his second volume of "Colenso on the Pentateuch." But if he does, he will be more fortunate than most owners of books. Pitiful are their thoughts as they look round their shelves. The silent friends of their youth, the acquisitions of their mature age, have departed. Even popular preachers cannot work miracles, like Thomas à Kempis, and pray back their borrowed volumes. As the Rev. Robert Elsmere says, "Miracles do not happen"—at least, to book-collectors.

"Murray sighs o'er Pope and Swift, and many a treasure more," said Cowper, when Lord Mansfield's house was burned, and we have all had experience of the sorrows of Murray. Even people who are not bibliophiles, nay, who class bibliophiles with "blue-and-white young men," know that a book in several volumes loses an unfair proportion of its usefulness, and almost all its value, when one or more of the volumes are gone. Grote's works, or Mill's, Carlyle's, or Milman's, seem nothing when they are incomplete. It always happens, somehow, that the very tome you want to consult is that which has fallen among borrowers. Even Panurge, who praised the race of borrowers so eloquently, could scarcely have found an excuse for the borrowers of books.

> "Tel est le triste sort de tout livre prêté,
> Souvent il est perdu, toujours il est gâté."

"Often lost, always spoiled," said Charles Nodier, "such is the fate of every book one lends." The Parisian collector, Guibert de

Pixérécourt, would lend no books at all to his dearest friends. His motto, inscribed above the lintel of his library-door, was, "Go to them that sell, and buy for yourselves." As Pixérécourt was the owner of many volumes which "they that sell" cannot procure, or which could only be bought at enormous rates, his caution (we will not say churlishness) was rather inconvenient for men of letters. But if hard pressed and in a strait, he would make his friend a gift of the book which was necessary to his studies. This course had the effect of preventing people from wishing to borrow. But many of the great collectors have been more generous than Pixérécourt. We forget the name (not an illustrious one) of the too good-natured man who labelled his books, "Not my own, but my friends'." "Sibi et amicis" ("His own and his friends' property") has been the motto of several illustrious amateurs since Grolier and Maioli stamped it on the beautifully decorated morocco of their bindings. Other people have invented book-plates, containing fell curses in doggrel Latin or the vernacular on the careless or dishonest borrower:

"A pice Pierrot pendu
Parceque librum non a rendu"

is the kind of macaronic French and Latin which schoolboys are accustomed to write under a sketch of the borrower expiating his offences on the gallows.

The mischief of borrowing, the persistent ill-luck which cleaves to property thus obtained, have been proverbial since the young prophet dropped the axe-head in the deep water, and cried, "Alas, for it is borrowed." The old prophet, readily altering the specific gravity of the article, enabled his disciple to regain it. But there are no prophets now, none, at least, who can repair our follies, and remove their baneful effects by a friendly miracle. What miracle can restore the books we borrow and lose, or the books we borrow and spoil with ink, or with candle-wax, or which children scrawl or paint over, or which "the dog ate," like the famous poll-book at an Irish election, that fell into the broth, and ultimately into the jaws of an illiterate animal? Books are such delicate things! Yet men—and still more frequently women —read them so close to the fire that the bindings warp, and start, and gape like the shells of a moribund oyster. Other people never have a paper-knife, and cut the leaves of books with cards, railway tickets, scissors, their own fingers, or any other weapon that chances to seem convenient. Then books are easily dirtied. A little dust falls into the leaves, and is smudged by the fingers. No fuller on earth can cleanse it. The art of man can remove certain sorts of stains, but only by stripping the book of its binding, and washing leaf by leaf in certain acids, an expensive and dangerous process. There are books for use, stout, everyday articles, and books for pious contemplation, original editions, or tomes that have belonged to great collectors. The borrower, who only wants to extract a passage of which he is in momentary need, is a person heedless of these distinctions. He enters a friend's house, or (for this sort of borrower thrives at college) a friend's rooms, seizes a first edition of Keats, or Shelley, or an Aldine Homer, or Elzevir Cæsar of the good date, and hurries away with it, leaving a hasty scrawl, "I have taken your Shelley," signed with initials. Perhaps the owner of the book never sees the note. Perhaps he does not recognize the hand. The borrower is just the man to forget the whole transaction. So there is a blank in the shelves, a gap among the orderly volumes, a blank never to be filled up, unless our amateur advertises his woes in the newspapers.

All borrowers are bad; but in this, as in other crimes, there are degrees. The man who acts as Ménage advises, in the aphorism which Garrick used as a motto on his bookplate, the man who reads a book instantly and promptly returns it, is the most pardonable borrower. But how few people do this! As a rule, the last thing the borrower thinks of is to read the book which he has secured. Or rather, that is the last thing but one; the very last idea that enters his mind is the project of returning the volume. It simply "lies about," and gets dusty in his rooms. A very bad borrower is he who makes pencil marks on books. Perhaps he is a little more excusable than the borrower who does not read at all.

A clean margin is worth all the marginalia of Poe, though he, to do him justice, seems chiefly to have written on volumes that were his own property. De Quincey, according to Mr. Hill Burton, appears to have lacked the faculty of mind which recognizes the duty of returning books. Mr. Hill Burton draws a picture of "Papaverius" living in a sort of cave or den, the walls of which were books, while books lay around in tubs. Who was to find a loved and lost tome in this vast accumulation? But De Quincey at least made good use of what he borrowed. The common borrower does nothing of the kind. Even Professor Mommsen, when he had borrowed manuscripts of great value in his possession, allowed his house to get itself set on fire. Europe lamented with him, but deepest was the wail of a certain college at Cambridge which had lent its treasures. Even Paul Louis Courier blotted horribly a Laurentian MS. of "Daphnis and Chloe." When Chénier lent his annotated "Malherbe," the borrower spilt a bottle of ink over it. Thinking of these things, of these terrible, irreparable calamities, the wonder is, not that men still lend, but that any one has the courage to borrow. It is more dreadful far to spoil or lose a friend's book than to have our own lost or spoiled. Stoicism easily submits to the latter sorrow, but there is no remedy for a conscience sensible of its own unlucky guilt.

CLUB BORES.

THE London Club has been sitting in a judicial way on one of its members. This member of the Club seems to have been what Thackeray's waiter called "a harbitrary gent." The servants of the club had to complain that he did not make "their lives so sweet to them that they (the servants) greatly cared to live," if we may parody Arthur's address to his erring queen. The Club has not made a vacancy in its ranks by requesting the arbitrary member to withdraw. But his conduct was deemed, on the report of the Committee, worthy of being considered by the Club. And that is always something. In an age when clubs are really almost universal, most men have had occasion to wish that their society would sit occasionally on some of the members. The member who bullies the servants is a not uncommon specimen of the club-bore. He may be called the bore truculent. He has been excellently caricatured by Thackeray in the " Book of Snobs."

There we have the club-bore who makes such a fuss about his chop, and scolds the waiter so terribly. "Look at it, sir; is it a chop for a gentleman? Smell it, sir; is it fit to put on a club table?" These, or such as these, are the words of the gallant terror of waiters. Now it is clearly unjust to make a waiter responsible for the errors, however grave, of a very different character, the cook. But this mistake the arbitrary gent is continually making. The cook is safe in his inaccessible stronghold, down below. He cannot be paraded for punishment on the quarter-deck, where Captain Bragg, of the Gunboat and Torpedo Club, exercises justice. Therefore the miserable waiter is rebuked in tones of thunder because the Captain's steak is underdone, or because Nature (or the market gardener) has not made the stalks of asparagus so green and succulent as their charming tops. People who do not know the scolding club-bore at home are apt to be thankful that they are not favoured with his intimate acquaintance, and are doubly grateful

that they are not members of his family.
For if, in a large and quiet room full of
strangers, a man can give loose to his temper
without provocation, and outroar the thunder,
what must this noisy person do at home?
"In an English family," says a social critic,
"the father is the man who shouts." How
the club-bore must shout when he is in his
own castle, surrounded only by his trembling
kindred and anxious retainers! In his castle
there is no one to resist or criticise him—
unless indeed his wife happen to be a lady,
like Clytemnestra, of masculine resolution.
In that case the arbitrary gent may be a
father of a family who is not allowed to shout
at home, but is obliged to give nature free
play by shouting abroad.

There are plenty of other club-bores besides
the man who rates these generally affable and
well-behaved persons, the club servants. One
of the worst is the man whom you never see
anywhere except at the club, and whom you
never fail to see there. It is bad enough
when you have no acquaintance with him.
Murders have probably been committed by
sensitive persons for no better reason (often
for worse reasons) than that they are tired

of seeing some one else going about. His voice, his manner, his cough, especially his cough, become unendurable. People who cough in clubs are generally amateurs of the art. They are huskier, more wheezing, more pertinacious in working away at a cough till they have made it a masterpiece than any other mortals. We believe that club Asthmats (it is quite as good a word as "Æsthetes") practise in the Reading Room of the British Museum, where they acquire their extraordinary compass and mastery of various notes. Be this as it may, the cough which drives every one but its owner out of the room (though doubtless an affliction to the proprietor) gives him rank as a club-bore of the finest water. The bore who always enters into conversation, though he has nothing to say, merely because you used to dislike him at school, or college, or elsewhere, is another common annoyance. The man who is engaged, apparently, on a large work, and who rushes about the library hunting for Proclus and Jamblichus when other occupants of the room wish to be quiet, is naturally detested.

Most men are the bores of some other person. People of watchful mind and intelligent habit, who talk in the drawing-room, are regarded as bores by fat old gentlemen who wish to sleep there. And as these gentlemen turn the drawing-room into a dormitory, which resounds with their snoring, they in turn are bores to people who wish to read the papers. But if these students drop the poker with a clang, or dash down small tables in order to waken the sleepers, they, in their turn, give a good deal of annoyance. The man who talks about politics at great length, is only one of the common bores of the world transported into a club. But the man with a voice which in ordinary conversation pierces through all the hum of voices, like a clarion note in battle, would be a bore anywhere. If he were in the wilderness of Sinai, he would annoy the monks in the convent near the top. His voice is one of those terrible, inscrutable scourges of nature, like the earthquake and the mosquito, which tax our poor human wisdom to reconcile with any monistic theory of the benevolent government of the universe. Once admit an evil principle, however, and the thing is clear. The club-bore with the trumpet tones, which he cannot moderate, is possessed, on this theory, by a fiend. As men are talking quietly of turnips in one corner of the room, of rent in another, and of racing in a third, his awful notes blend in from the fourth corner with strident remarks on Bulgarian philology.

The ancient Greeks were well accustomed to club life, for each of their little cities was only a large club. They had, therefore, to deal with the problem of bores. Some of them, consequently, had the institution of annually devoting to the infernal gods the most unpopular citizens. These persons were called *catharmata*, which may be freely translated "scapegoats." Could not clubs annually devote one or more scapebores to the infernal gods? They might ballot for them, of course, on some merciful and lenient principle. One white ball in ten or twenty black ones might enable the bore to keep his membership for the next year. The warning, if he only escaped this species of ostracism very narrowly, might do him a great deal of moral good. Of course the process would be unpleasant, but it is seldom agreeable to be done good to. Occasionally even the most good-natured members would stand apart, not voting, or even would place the black ball in the mystic urn. Then the scapebore would have his subscription returned to him, and would be obliged to seek in other haunts servants to swear at, and sofas to snore on. Another suggestion, that members should be balloted for anew every five years, would simply cause clubs to be depopulated. Pall-Mall and St. James's would be desolate, mourning their children, and refusing comfort. The system would act like a proscription. People would give up their friends that they might purchase aid against their enemies. Clubs are more endurable as they are, though members do suffer grievously from the garrulity, the coughs, the slumbrous tendencies, and the temper of their fellow-men.

PHIZ.

Mr. Hablot K. Browne, better known as Phiz, was an artist of a departed school to whom we all owe a great deal of amusement. He was not so versatile nor so original as Cruickshank; he had not the genius, nor the geniality, still less the sense of beauty, of John Leech. In his later years his work became more and more unequal, till he was sometimes almost as apt to scribble hasty scrawls as Constantin Guys. M. Guys was an artist selected by M. Baudelaire as the fine flower of modern art, and the true, though hurried, designer of the fugitive modern beauty. It is recorded that M. Guys was once sent to draw a scene of triumph and certain illuminations in London, probably about the end of the Crimean War. His sketch did not reach the office of the paper for which he worked in time, and some one went to see what the man of genius was doing. He was found in bed, but he was equal to the occasion. Snatching a sheet of paper and a pencil he drew a curve. "There," said he, "is the triumphal arch, and here"—scribbling a number of scratches like eccentric comets—"here are the fireworks." Mr. Browne's drawings occasionally showed a tendency to approach the rudimentary sort of "pictograph" rather than give what a dramatic critic calls "a solid and studied rendering" of events. But many of Mr. Browne's illustrations of Dickens are immortal. They are closely bound up with our earliest and latest recollections of the work of the "incomparable Boz." Mr. Pickwick, we believe, was not wholly due to the fancy of Mr. Browne, but of the unfortunate Seymour, whom death prevented from continuing the series. Every one has heard how Mr. Thackeray, then an unknown man, wished to illustrate one of Mr. Dickens's early stories, and brought Mr. Dickens examples of his skill. Fortunately, his offer was not accepted. Mr. Thackeray's pencil was the proper ally of his pen. He saw and drew Costigan, Becky, Emmy, Lord Steyne, as no one else could have drawn them. But he had not beheld the creations of Boz in the same light of imaginative vision. Sometimes, too, it must be allowed that Mr. Thackeray drew very badly. His "Peg of Limavaddy," in the "Irish Sketch Book," is a most formless lady, and by no means justifies the enthusiasm of her poet. Thus the task of illustrating "Pickwick" fell to Mr. Browne, and he carried on the conceptions of his predecessor with extraordinary vigour. The old vein of exaggerated caricature he inherited from the taste of an elder generation. But making allowance for the exaggeration, what can be better than Mr. Pickwick sliding, or the awful punishment of Stiggins at the hands of the long-suffering Weller? We might wish that the young lady in fur-topped boots was prettier, and indeed more of a lady. But Mr. Browne never had much success, we think, in drawing pretty faces. He tried to improve in this respect, but either his girls had little character, or the standard of female beauty has altered. As to this latter change, there can be no doubt at all. Leech's girls are not like Thackeray's early pictures of women; and Mr. Du Maurier's are sometimes sicklied o'er with the pale cast of an æsthetic period.

It is probable that the influence of Mr. Browne's art reacted in some degree on Dickens. In the old times every one whom the author invented the artist was pretty certain to caricature. Thus the author may have felt the temptation to keep pace with the frolic humour of the artist. Mr. Browne cannot be blamed for a tendency to exaggerate noses and other features, which was almost universal in his time. None of us can say what conception would now be entertained of Dickens's characters if Mr. Browne had not drawn them. In the later works of Dickens (when they were illustrated) other artists were employed, as Mr. Stone and Mr. Fildes. These are accomplished painters of established reputation, and they of course avoided the old system of caricature, the old forced humour. But we doubt whether their designs are so intimately associated with the persons in the stories as are the designs of Mr. Browne. The later artists had this disadvantage, that the later novels (except "Great Expectations," which was not illustrated) were neither so good nor so popular as "Pickwick," "Nicholas Nickleby," "Martin Chuzzlewit," "David Copperfield," or even "Bleak House." We never can have any Mr. Micawber but Phiz's indescribably jaunty Micawber. His Mr. Pecksniff is not very like a human being, but his collars and his eye-glass redeem him, and after all Pecksniff is a transcendental and incredible Tartuffe. Tom Pinch is even less sympathetic in the drawings than in the novel. Jonas Chuzzlewit is also "too steep," as a modern critic has said in modern slang. But in the novel, too, Mr. Jonas is somewhat precipitous. Nicholas Nickleby is a colourless sort of young man in the illustrations, but then he is not very vividly presented in the text. Ralph Nickleby and Arthur Gride may pair off with Jonas Chuzzlewit, but who can disparage the immortal Mr. Squeers? From the first moment when we see him at his inn, with the starveling little boys, through all the story, Mr. Squeers is consistently exquisite. In spite of his cruelty, coarseness, hypocrisy, there is a kind of humour in Mr. Squeers which makes him not quite detestable. In "David Copperfield" Mr. Micawber is perhaps the only artistic creation of much permanent merit, unless it be the waiter who consumed David's dinner, and the landlady who gave him a pint of the Regular Stunning.

In "Bleak House" Mr. Browne made some credible attempts to be tragic and pathetic. Jo is remembered, and the gateway of the churchyard where the rats were, and the Ghost's Walk in the gloomy domain of Lady Dedlock.

It is a singular and gloomy feature in the character of young ladies and gentlemen of a particular type that they have ceased to care for Dickens, as they have ceased to care for Scott. They say they cannot read Dickens. When Mr. Pickwick's adventures are presented to the modern maid, she behaves like the Cambridge freshman. "Euclide viso, cohorruit et evasit." When he was shown Euclid he evinced dismay, and sneaked off. Even so do most young people act when they are expected to read "Nicholas Nickleby" and "Martin Chuzzlewit." They call these masterpieces "too gutterly gutter;" they cannot sympathize with this honest humour and conscious pathos. Consequently the innumerable references to Sam Weller, and Mrs. Gamp, and Mr. Pecksniff, and Mr. Winkle which fill our ephemeral literature are written for these persons in an unknown tongue. The number of people who could take a good pass in Mr. Calverley's Pickwick Examination Paper is said to be diminishing. Pathetic questions are sometimes put. Are we not too much cultivated? Can this fastidiousness be anything but a casual passing phase of taste? Are all people over thirty who cling to their Dickens and their Scott old fogies? Are we wrong in preferring them to " Bootle's Baby," and " The Quick or the Dead," and the novels of M. Paul Bourget?

THEORY AND PRACTICE OF PROPOSALS.

THERE is no subject in the whole range of human affairs so interesting to a working majority of the race as the theory and practice of proposals of marriage. Men perhaps cease to be very much concerned about the ordeal when they have been through it. But the topic never loses its charm for the fair, though they are presumed only to wait and to listen, and never to speak for themselves. That this theory has its exceptions appears to be the conviction of many novelists. They not only make their young ladies "lead up to it," but heroines occasionally go much further than that, and do more than prompt an inexperienced wooer. But all these things are only known to the world through the confessions of novelists, who, perhaps, themselves receive confessions. M. Goncourt not long ago requested all his fair readers to send him notes of their own private experience. How did you feel when you were confirmed? How did Alphonse whisper his passion? These and other questions, quite as intimate, were set by M. Goncourt. He meant to use the answers, with all discreet reserve, in his next novel. Do English novelists receive any private information, and if they do not, how are we to reconcile their knowledge—they are all love-adepts—with the morality of their lives? "We live like other people, only more purely," says the author of "Some Private Views," which is all very well. No man is bound to incriminate himself. But as in the course of his career a successful novelist describes many hundreds of proposals, all different, are we to believe that he is so prompted merely by imagination? Are there no "documents," as M. Zola says, for all this prodigious deal of love-making? These are questions which await a reply in the interests of ethics and of art. Meanwhile an editor of enterprise has selected five-and-thirty separate examples of "popping the question," as he calls it, from the tomes of British fiction. To begin with an early case—when

Tom Jones returned to his tolerant Sophia, he called her "Madam," and she called him "Mr. Jones," not Tom. She asked Thomas how she could rely on his constancy, when the lover of Miss Segrim drew a mirror from his pocket (like Strephon in "Iolanthe"), and cried, "Behold that lovely figure, that shape, those eyes," with other compliments; "can the man who shall be in possession of these be inconstant?" Sophia was charmed by the "man in possession," but forced her features into a frown. Presently Thomas "caught her in his arms," and the rest was in accordance with what Mr. Trollope and the best authorities recommend. How differently did Arthur Pendennis carry himself when he proposed to Laura, and did not want to be accepted! Lord Farintosh—his affecting adventure is published here—proposed nicely enough, but did not behave at all well when he was rejected. By the way, when young men in novels are not accepted, they invariably ask the lady whether she loves another. Only young ladies, and young men whom they have rejected, know whether this is common in real life. It does not seem quite right.

Kneeling has probably gone out, though

Mr. Jingle knelt before the maiden aunt, and remained in that attitude for no less than five minutes. In Mr. Howell's "Modern Instance," kneeling was not necessary, and the heroine kept thrusting her face into her lover's necktie; so the author tells us. M. Théophile Gautier says that ladies invariably lay their heads on the shoulder of the man who proposes (if he is the right man), and for this piece of "business" (as we regret to say he considers it) he assigns various motives. But he was a Frenchman, and the cynicism of that nation (to parody a speech of Tom Jones's) cannot understand the delicacy of ours. Mr. Blackmore (in "Lorna Doone") lets his lover make quite a neat and appropriate speech, but that was in the seventeenth century. When Artemus Ward began a harangue of this sort, Betsy Jane knocked him off the fence on which he was sitting, and first criticising his eloquence in a trenchant style, added, "If you mean being hitched, I'm in it." In other respects the lover of Lorna Doone behaved as the best authorities recommend.

Mr. Whyte Melville ventured to describe Chastelard's proposal to Mary Stuart, but it was not exactly in Mr. Swinburne's manner, and, where historical opinions disagree, no reliance can be placed on speeches which were not taken down by the intelligent reporters. Mr. Slope had his ears boxed when he proposed to Mrs. Bold, but such Amazonian conduct is probably rare, and neither party is apt to boast of it. He also, being accepted, behaved in the manner to which the highest authorities have lent their sanction, or, at least, he meant to do so, when the lady "fled like a roe to her chamber." For all widows are not like widow Malone (ochone!) renowned in song. When Arbaces, the magician, proposed to Ione, he did so in the most necromantic and hierophantic manner in which it could be done; his "properties" including a statue of Isis, an altar, "and a quick, blue, darting, irregular flame." But his flame, quick, blue, darting, and irregular as it was, lighted no answering blaze in the ice-cold breast of the lovely Ione. When rejected (in spite of a splendid arrangement of magic lanterns, then a novelty, got up regardless of expense) Arbaces swore like an intoxicated mariner, rather than a necromaunt accustomed to move in the highest circles and pentacles. Nancy, Miss Broughton's heroine, tells her middle-aged wooer, among other things, that she accepts him, because "I did think it would be nice for the boys; but I like you myself, besides." After this ardent confession, he "kissed her with a sort of diffidence." Many men would have preferred to go out and kick "the boys."

Mr. Rochester's proposal to Jane Eyre should be read in the works both of Bret Harte and of Miss Brontë. We own that we prefer Bret Harte's Mr. Rawjester, who wearily ran the poker through his hair, and wiped his boots on the dress of his beloved. Even in the original authority, Mr. Rochester conducted himself rather like a wild beast. He "ground his teeth," "he seemed to devour" Miss Eyre "with his flaming glance." Miss Eyre behaved with sense. "I retired to the door." Proposals of this desperate and homicidal character are probably rare in real life, or, at least, out of lunatic asylums. To be sure, Mr. Rochester's house *was* a kind of lunatic asylum.

Adam Bede's proposal to Dinah was a very thoughtful, earnest proposal. John Inglesant himself could not have been less like that victorious rascal, Tom Jones. Colonel Jack, on the other hand, "used no great ceremony." But Colonel Jack, like the woman of Samaria in the Scotch minister's sermon, "had enjoyed a large and rich matrimonial experience," and went straight to the point, being married the very day of his successful wooing. Some one in a story of Mr. Wilkie Collins's asks the fatal question at a croquet party. At lawn-tennis, as Nimrod said long ago, "the pace is too good to inquire" into matters of the affections. In Sir Walter's golden prime, or rather in the Forty-five as Sir Walter understood it, ladies were in no hurry, and could select elegant expressions. Thus did Flora reply to Waverley, "I can but explain to you with candour the feelings which I now entertain; how they might be altered by a train of circumstances too favourable, perhaps, to be hoped for, it were in vain even to conjecture; only be assured, Mr. Waverley, that after my brother's honour and happiness, there is none which I shall more sincerely pray for than yours." This love is indeed what Sidney Smith heard the Scotch lady call "love in the abstract." Mr. Kingsley's Tom Thurnall somehow proposed, was accepted, and was "converted" all at once—a more complex crototheological performance was never heard of before.

Many of Mr. Abell's thirty-five cases are selected from novelists of no great mark; it would have been more instructive to examine only the treatment of the great masters of romance. But, after all, this is of little consequence. All day long and every day novelists are teaching the "Art of Love," and playing Ovid to the time. But what are novels without love? Mere waste paper, only fit to be reduced to pulp, and restored to a whiteness and firmness on which more love lessons may be written.*

* These remarks were made before the great discovery of some modern authors, that the best novels are those in which there is never a petticoat.

MASTER SAMUEL PEPYS.

No man is a hero to his valet, and unluckily Samuel Pepys, by way of a valet, chose posterity. All the trifles of temper, habit, vice, and social ways which a keen-eyed valet may observe in his master Samuel Pepys carefully recorded about himself, and bequeathed to the diversion of future generations. The world knows Pepys as the only man who ever wrote honest confessions, for Rousseau could not possibly be candid for five minutes together, and St. Augustine was heavily handicapped by being a saint. Samuel Pepys was no saint. We might best define him, perhaps, by saying that if ever any man was his own Boswell, that man was Samuel Pepys. He had Bozzy's delightful appreciation of life; writing in cypher, he had Bozzy's shamelessness and more, and he was his own hero.

It is for these qualities and achievements that he received a monument honoured in St. Olave's, his favourite church. In St. Olave's, on December 23, 1660, Samuel went to pray, and had his pew all covered with rosemary and baize. Thence he went home, and "with much ado made haste to spit a turkey." Here, in St. Olave's, he listened to "a dull sermon from a stranger." Here, when "a Scot" preached, Pepys "slept all the sermon," as a man who could "never be reconciled to the voice of the Scot." What an unworthy prejudice! Often he writes, "After a dull sermon of the Scotchman, home;" or to church again, "and there a simple coxcombe preached worse than the Scot." Frequently have the sacred walls of St. Olave's, where his effigy may be seen, echoed to the honest snoring of the Clerk of the Navy. There Pepys lies now, his body having been brought "in a very honourable and solemn manner," from Clapham, where, according to that respected sheet, the *Post-boy*, he expired on May 26, 1703. No stone marked the spot, when Mr. Mynors Bright's delightful edition of Pepys was published in 1875.

Now Pepys is honoured in that church where he sleeps even sounder than in days when the Scot preached worse than usual. But he is rewarded in death—not, it may be feared, for his real services to England, but because he has amused us all so much. A dead humorist may be better than a living official, however honest, industrious, and careful.

In all these higher things Pepys was not found wanting. The son of a tailor in the City, he yet had connections of good family, who were of service to him when he entered public life. Samuel Pepys was born in 1632. He was educated at Magdalene, Cambridge where he was once common-roomed for being "scandalously overserved with liquor." Through life he retained a friendly admiration of Magdalene strong ale. He married a girl of fifteen when he was but twenty-two; he entered the service of the State shortly afterwards. He was the Chief Secretary for Naval Affairs during many years; he defended his department at the Bar of the House of Commons after De Ruyter's attack in 1668, and he remained true to the Stuart dynasty in heart after James was driven abroad. Yet, though his contemporary biographer calls Pepys the greatest and most useful public servant that ever filled the same situations in England, Pepys would not now be honoured if he had not kept the most amusing diary in the world. Samuel was a highly conscientious, truly pious man, constant in all religious exercises, though he did slumber when the Scot wagged his pow in a pulpit. At the same time, Samuel lived in a very fast age, an age when pleasure was a business, and "old Rowley, the king," led the brawls. He was young when society was most scandalously diverting. He had a pretty wife, "poor wretch," of whom he stood in some awe; and yet this inconsistent naval secretary liked to flit from flower to flower. He was vain, greedy, wanton, fond of the delight of the eye and the pride of life; he was loving and loose in his manners; he was pious, repentant, profligate; and he deliberately told the whole tale of all his many changes of mood and mistress, of piety and pleasure. One cannot open Pepys at random without finding him at his delightful old games. On the Lord's day he goes to church with Mr. Creed, and hears a good sermon from the red-faced parson. He came home, read divinity, dined, and, he says, 'played the fool," and won a quart of sack from Mr. Creed. Then to supper at the Banquet House, and there Mr. Pepys and his wife fell to quarrelling over the beauty of Mrs. Pierce; "she against, and I for," says superfluous Pepys. No one is in the least likely to suspect that Mrs. Pepys was angry with her lord because he did not think Mrs. Pierce a beauty.

How living the whole story is! One can smell the flowers of that Sunday in May, and the roast beef. The sack seems but newly drawn, the red cheeks of Mrs. Pierce as fresh as ever. The flowers grow over them now, or the church floor covers them; the sack is drunk, the roast beef is eaten, the quarrel is over; the beauty and the red-faced parson, the husband and wife, they are all with Tullus and Ancus. *Pulvis et umbra*—that is the moral of "Pepys's Diary." Life yet lives so strong in the cyphered pages; all the colour, all the mirth, all the little troubles and sins, and vows, they are so real they might be of yesterday or to-day, but the end of them came nigh two hundred years ago. Therefore, to read Pepys is to enjoy our own brief innings better, as men who know that our March is passing where Pepys' May has flown before, and that we shall soon be with him and his wife, and the Scot, and the red-faced parson. So fleeting is life, whose record outlives it for ever; so brief, so swift, so faint the joys and sorrows, and all that we make marvel of in our own fortunes and those of other men.

Reading Pepys is thus like reading Montaigne, whose cheery scepticism his revelations recall. But Pepys has all the advantage of the man living in the busiest world over the recluse in that famed library, with the mottoes on the wall. Montaigne wrote in a retired and contemplative home, viewing life, as Osman Digna has viewed strife, "from afar," almost safe from the shots of fortune. But Pepys writes day by day, like a war correspondent, in the thick of the battle; his head "full of business," as he declares; his heart full of many desires, many covetings, much pride in matters that look small enough. He notes how, by chewing tobacco, Mr. Chetwynde, who was consumptive, became very fat. He remarks how a board fell, and the dust powdered the ladies' heads at the play, "which made good sport." He records every venison-pasty, every flagon of wine, every pretty wench whom he encountered in his march through his youth towards the vault in St. Olave's. He is vexed with Mrs. Pepys and troubled by "my aunt's base ugly humours." He is "full of repentance," like the Bad Man in the Ethics, and thinks how much he is addicted to expense and pleasure, "so that now I can hardly reclaim myself." He interests himself in Dr. Williams's remarkable dog, which not only killed cats, but buried them with punctilious obsequies, never leaving the tip of puss's tail out of the ground. Then he goes to the play, "after swearing to my wife that I would never go to the play without her." He remembers one night that he passed "with the greatest epicurism of sleep," because he was often disturbed, and so got out of sleeping more conscious enjoyment. Now he sleeps what Socrates calls the sweetest slumber of all, if it be but dreamless, or, somewhere, he enjoys all new experience, with the lusty appetite of old.

INVOLUNTARY BAILEES.

LORD TENNYSON is probably the most extensive Involuntary Bailee at present living. The term "Involuntary Bailee" may or may not be a correct piece of legal terminology; at all events, it sounds very imposing, and can be easily explained.

An Involuntary Bailee is a person to whom people (generally unknown to him) send things which he does not wish to receive but which they are anxious to have returned. Most of us in our humble way are or have been Involuntary Bailees. When some one you meet at dinner recommends to your notice a book (generally of verse), and kindly insists on sending it to you next day by post as a loan, you are an Involuntary Bailee. You have the wretched book in your possession; no inducement would make you read it, and to pack it up and send it back again requires a piece of string, energy, brown paper, and stamps enough to defray the postage. Now, surely no casual acquaintance or neighbour for an hour at a dinner-party has any right thus to make demands on a man's energy, money, time, brown paper, string, and other capital and commodities.

If the book be sent as a present, the crime is less black, though still very culpable. You need take no notice of the present, whereby you probably offend the author for life, and thus get rid of him anyhow. Commonly, he is a minor poet, and sends you his tragedy on John Huss; or he is a writer on mythological subjects, and is anxious to weary you with a theory that Jack the Giant Killer was Julius Cæsar. At the worst, you can toss his gift into the waste-paper basket, or sell it for fourpence three-farthings, or set it on your bookshelf so as to keep the damp away from books of which you are not the Involuntary Bailee, but the unhappy purchaser. The case becomes truly black, as we have said, when the uncalled-for tribute has to be returned. Then it is sure to be lost, when the lender writes to say he wishes to recover it. In future he will go about telling people that the recipient stole his best ideas from the manuscript (if it was a manuscript) which he pretends to have lost.

Lord Tennyson has suffered from all these troubles to an extent which the average Bailee can only fancy by looking with his mind's eye through "patent double million magnifiers." A man so eminent as the Laureate is the butt of all the miserable minor poets, all the enthusiastic school-girls, all the autograph-hunters, all the begging-letter writers, all the ambitious young tragedians, and all the utterly unheard-of and imaginary relations in Kamschatka or Vancouver's Island with whom the wide world teems. Lord Tennyson has endured these people for some fifty years, and now he takes a decided line. He will not answer their letters, nor return their manuscripts.

Lord Tennyson is perfectly right to assume this attitude, only it makes life even more hideous than of old to Mr. Browning and Mr. Swinburne. Probably these distinguished writers are already sufficiently pestered by the Mr. Tootses of this world, whose chief amusement is to address epistles to persons of distinction. Mr. Toots was believed to answer his own letters himself, but the beings who fill Lord Tennyson's, and Mr. Gladstone's, and probably Mr. Browning's letter-box expect to receive answers. Frightened away from Lord Tennyson's baronial portals, they will now crowd thicker than ever round the gates of other poets who have not yet announced that they will prove irresponsive. Cannot the Company of Authors (if that be the correct style and title) take this matter up and succour the profession? Next, of course, to the baneful publisher and the hopelessly indifferent public, most authors suffer more from no one than from the unknown correspondent. The unknown correspondent is very frequently of the fair sex, and her bright home is not unusually in the setting sun. "Dear Mr. Brown," she writes to some poor author who never heard of her, nor of Idaho, in the States, where she lives, "I cannot tell you how much I admire your monograph on Phonetic Decay in its influence on Logic. Please send me two copies with autograph inscriptions. I hope to see you at home when I visit Europe in the Fall."

Every man of letters, however humble, is accustomed to these salutations, and probably

Lord Tennyson receives scores every morning at breakfast. Like all distinguished poets, like Scott certainly, we presume that he is annoyed with huge parcels of MSS. These (unless Lord Tennyson is more fortunate than other singers) he is asked to read, correct, and return with a carefully considered opinion as to the sender's chance of having "Assur ban-i-pal," a tragedy, accepted at the Gaiety Theatre. Rival but unheard-of bards will entreat him to use his influence to get their verses published. Others (all the world knows) will send him "spiteful letters," assuring him that "his fame in song has done them much wrong." How interesting it would be to ascertain the name of the author of that immortal "spiteful letter"! Probably many persons have felt that they could make a good guess; no less probably they have been mistaken.

In no way can the recipient avoid making enemies of the authors of all these communications if he is at all an honest, irascible man. Mr. Dickens used to reply to total strangers, and to poets like Miss Ada Menken, with a dignified and sympathetic politeness which disarmed wrath. But he probably thereby did but invite fresh trouble of the same kind. Mr. Thackeray (if a recently-published answer was a fair specimen) used to answer more briefly and brusquely. One thing is certain. No criticism not entirely laudatory, which the Involuntary Bailee may make of his correspondent's MS., will be accepted without remonstrance. Doubtless Lord Tennyson has at last chosen the only path of safety by declining to answer his unknown correspondents, or to return their rubbish, any more.

Of course, it is a wholly different affair when the anonymous correspondent sends several brace of grouse, or a salmon of noble proportions, or rare old books bound by Derome, or a service of Worcester china with the square mark, or other tribute of that kind. Probably some dozen of rhymers sent Lord Tennyson amateur congratulatory odes when he was raised to the peerage. If he is at all like other poets, he would have preferred a few dozen of extremely curious old port, or a Villon published by Galiot du Pré, or a gold nugget, or some of the produce of the diamond mines, to any number of signed congratulations from total strangers. Actors seem to receive nicer tributes than poets. Two brace of grouse were thrown on the stage when Mr. Irving was acting in a northern town. This is as picturesque as, and a great deal more permanently enjoyable than, a shower of flowers and wreaths. Another day a lady threw a gold cross on the stage, and yet another enthusiast contributed rare books appropriately bound. These gifts will not, of course, be returned by a celebrity who respects himself; but they bless him who gives and him who takes, much more than tons of manuscript poetry, and thousands of entreaties for an autograph, and millions of announcements that the writer will be "proud to drink your honour's noble health."

SUMMER NIGHTS.

If the best of all ways of lengthening our days be to take a few hours from the night, many of us are involuntarily prolonging existence at the present hour. Macbeth did not murder sleep more effectually than the hot weather does. At best, in the sultry nights, most people sleep what is called "a dog's sleep," and by no means the sleep of a lucky dog. As the old English writers say, taking a distinction which our language appears to have lost, we "rather slumber than sleep," waking often, and full of the foolishest of dreams. This condition of things probably affects politics and society more than the thoughtless suppose. If literature produced in the warm, airless fog of July be dull, who can marvel thereat?

"Of all gods," says Pausanias, "Sleep is dearest to the Muses;" and when the child of the Muses does not get his regular nine hours' rest (which he fails to do in warm weather), then his verse and prose are certain to bear traces of his languor. It is true that all children of the Muses do not require about double the allowance of the saints. Five hours was all St. Jerome took, and probably Byron did not sleep much more during the season when he wrote "Childe Harold." The moderns who agree with the Locrians in erecting altars to Sleep, can only reply that probably "Childe Harold" would have been a better poem if Byron had kept more regular hours when he was composing it. So far they will, perhaps, have Mr. Swinburne with them, though that author also has Sung before Sunrise, when he would (if the wisdom of the ancients be correct) have been better employed in plucking the flower of sleep.

Leaving literature, and looking at society, it is certain that the human temper is more lively, and more unkind things are said, in a sultry than in a temperate season. In the restless night-watches people have time to brood over small wrongs, and wax indignant over tiny slights and unoffered invitations. Perhaps politics, too, are apt to be more rancorous in a "heated term." Man is very much what his liver makes him.

Hot weather vexes the unrested soul in nothing more than this, that (like a revolution in Paris) it tempts the people to "go down into the streets." The streets are cooler, at least, than stuffy gas-lit rooms; and if the public would only roam them in a contemplative spirit, with eyes turned up to the peaceful constellations, the public might fall down an area now and then, but would not much disturb the neighbourhood. But the 'Arry that walketh by night thinks of nothing less than admiring, with Kant, the starry heavens and the moral nature of man. He seeks his peers, and together in great bands they loiter or run, stopping to chaff each other, and to jeer at the passer-by. Their satire is monotonous in character, chiefly consisting of the words for using which the famous Mr. Budd beat the baker.* Now, the sultry weather makes it absolutely necessary to leave bedroom windows wide open, so that he who is courting sleep has all the advantage of studying the dialogue of the slums. These disturbances last till two in the morn-

* What *was* this anecdote?

ing in some otherwise quiet districts near the river. When Battersea 'Arry has been "on the fly" in Chelsea, while Chelsea 'Arry has been pursuing pleasure in Battersea, the homeward-faring bands meet, about one in the morning, on the Embankment. Then does Cheyne Walk hear the amœbean dialogues of strayed revellers, and knows not whether Battersea or Chelsea best deserves the pipe, the short black pipe, for which the rival swains compete in profanity and slang. In music, too, does this modern Dionysiac procession rejoice, and Kensington echoes like Cithæron when Pan was keeping his orgies there—Pan and the Theban nymphs. The music and the song of the London street roamer is excessively harsh, crabbed, and tuneless. Almost as provoking it is, in a quiet way, when three or four quite harmless people meet under a bedroom window and converse in their usual tone of voice about their private affairs.

These little gatherings sometimes seem as if they would never break up, and though the persons in the piece mean no harm, they are nearly as noxious to sleep as the loud musical water-side rough or public-house loafer. Dogs, too, like men, seem to feel it incumbent on them to howl more than usual in hot weather, and to bay the moon with particular earnestness in July. No enemy of sleep is deadlier than a dear, good, affectionate dog, whose owners next door have accidentally shut him out. The whole night long he bewails his loneliness, in accents charged with profound melancholy. The author of the "Amusement Philosophique" would have us believe that animals can speak. Nothing makes more for his opinion than the exquisite variety of lyrical howl in which a shut-out dog expresses every phrase of blighted affection, incommunicable longing, and supreme despair. Somehow he never, literally never, wakens his owners. He only keeps all the other people in a four-mile radius wide awake. Yet how few have the energy and public spirit to get up and go for that dog with sticks, umbrellas, and pieces of road-metal! The most enterprising do little more than shout at him out of the window, or take long futile shots at him with bits of coal from the fireplace. When we have a Municipal Government of London, then, perhaps, measures will be taken with dogs, and justice will be meted out to the owners of fowls. At present these fiends in human shape can keep their detestable pets, and defy the menaces, as they have rejected the prayers, of their neighbours. The amount of profanity, insanity, ill-health, and general misery which one rooster can cause is far beyond calculation.

When London nights are intolerable, people think with longing of the cool, fragrant country, of the jasmine-muffled lattices, and the groups beneath the dreaming evening star. One dreams of coffee after dinner in the open air, as described in "In Memoriam;" one longs for the cool, the hush, the quiet. But try the country on a July night. First you have trouble with all the great, big, hairy, leathery moths and bats which fly in at the jasmine-muffled lattice, and endeavour to put out your candle. You blow the candle out, and then a bluebottle fly in good voice comes out too, and is accompanied by very fair imitations of mosquitoes. Probably they are only gnats, but in blowing their terrible little trumpets they are of the mosquito kind. Next the fact dawns on you that the church clock in the neighbouring spire strikes the quarters, and you know that you cannot fall asleep before the chime wakes you up again, with its warning, "Another quarter gone." The cocks come forth and crow about four; the hens proclaim to a drowsy world that they have fulfilled the duties of maternity. All through the ambrosial night three cows, in the meadow under your windows, have been lamenting the loss of their calves. Of all terrible notes, the "routing" of a bereaved, or amorous, or homesick cow is the most disturbing. It carries for miles, and keeps all who hear it—all town-bred folk, at least—far from the land of Nod. At dawn the song-birds begin, and hold you awake, as they disturbed Rufinus long ago; but the odds are that they do not inspire you, like Rufinus, with the desire to write poetry. The short and simple language of profanity is more likely to come unbidden to the wakeful lips. Thus, as John Leech found out, the country in July is almost as dreadful at night as the town. Nay, thanks to the cow, we think the country may bear away the prize for all that is uncomfortable, all that is hostile to sleep and the Muses. Yet rustics always sleep very well, and no more mind the noise of cocks, sparrows, cows, dogs, and ducks than the owner of a town-bred dog minds when his faithful hound drives a whole street beyond their patience. It is a matter of sound health and untaxed brains. If we always gave our minds a rest, none of us would dread the noises of the nights of summer.

ON HYPOCHONDRIACS.

A NICE state we are in, according to the *Medical Times*. If the secrets of our "case-books"—that is, we suppose, our medical *dossiers*, doctors' records of the condition of their patients—could be revealed, it would be shown that many clever people have a fancy skeleton in their cupboards. By a fancy skeleton we mean, not some dismal secret of crime or shame, but a melancholy and apprehensiveness without any ground in outward facts. With the real skeleton doctors have nothing to do. He rather belongs to the province of Scotland Yard. If a man has compromised himself in some way, if he has been found out by some scoundrel, if he is compelled to "sing," as the French say, or to pay "blackmail," then the doctor is not concerned in the business. A detective, a revolver, or a well-planned secret flight may be prescribed to the victim. Other real skeletons men possess which do not come of their own misdeeds. One of their friends or one of their family may be the skeleton, or the consciousness of coming and veritable misfortune, pecuniary or what-not. But the *Medical Times*, which no doubt ought to know, refers purely to cases of vague melancholy and hypochondriac foreboding. Apparently "The Spleen," the "English Disease," is as bad now as when Green wrote in verse and Dr. Cheyne in prose. Prosperous business men, literary gents in active employment, artists, students, tradesmen, "are all visited by melancholy, revealed only to their doctors, and sometimes to their domestic circle."

Unhappy domestic circle, brooded over by a gloomy parent, who thinks that life is too short, or faith too much a matter of speculation, or that the country is going to the dogs! Then the doctor, it seems, hears his patient, and recommends him only to drink a very little whisky and potash water, or to take two bottles of port every day, or to take to angling, or to give up smoking, or to work less or to work more, or to go to bed early or to get up late, or to ride, or to fence, or to play golf, or to go to Upper Egypt or the Engadine, or anything that fancy may dictate and opportunity suggest. So the kind physician advises his mournful self-tormentor, and then he himself flies round the corner and consults some brother-healer about his own subjective gloom.

Old ladies, in speaking of the misdeeds of youth, are apt to recommend "a good shaking" as a panacea. Really those victims of whom our contemporary speaks, appear to be persons on whom "a good shaking," mental or physical, would produce a salutary effect. Cowardice, vanity, overweening self-consciousness, are the causes of most melancholy. No doubt it has physical causes too. Dr. Johnson suffered,—one of the best and bravest of men. But most of us suffer—if suffer we do —because we over-estimate ourselves and our own importance. Mr. Matthew Arnold has tried to enforce this lesson. After a horrible murder in a railway carriage, Mr. Arnold observed, with pain, the "almost bloodthirsty clinging to life" of his fellow-passengers. In vain he pointed out to them that even if they were to depart, "the great mundane movement" would go on as usual. But they refused to be comforted. Every man was afraid of meeting his own Müller; and as to the great mundane movement, no one cared a pin. This selfishness is among the chief causes of melancholy. A man persuades himself that he will not live long, or that his prospects in this world or the next are gloomy; or he takes views as absurdly far-reaching as those of the spinsters in the old tale, who wept over the hypothetical fate of the child one of them might have had if she had been married. Now, there is a certain melancholy not unbecoming a man; indeed, to be without it is hardly to be human. Here we do find ourselves, indeed, like the shipwrecked mariner on the isle of Pascal's apologue; all around us are the unknown seas, all about us are the indomitable and eternal processes of generation and corruption. "We come like water, and like wind we go." Life is, indeed, as the great Persian says—

> "A moment's halt, a momentary taste
> Of being from the well beside the waste."

These just causes of melancholy and of awe have presented themselves to all reflective men at all times. They deeply affect the thought, so wholesome and so human, of Homer. They express themselves in that old English pagan's allegory of the bird that flies from the dark into the warm and lighted hall, and from the hall into the dark again. Not to be capable of these reflections is to be incapable of tasting the noblest poetry. Such thoughts actually give zest to our days, and sharpen our enjoyment of that which we have only a brief moment to enjoy. Such thoughts add their own sweetness and sadness to the song of the nightingale, to the fall of the leaves, to the coming of the spring. Were we "exempt from eld and age," this noble melancholy could never be ours, and we, like the ancient classical gods, would be incapable of tears. What Prometheus says in Mr. Bridge's poem is true—

> "Not in heaven,
> Among our easy gods, hath facile time
> A touch so keen to wake such love of life
> As stirs the frail and careful being of Man."

Such are the benefits of Melancholy, when she is only an occasional guest, and is not pampered or made the object of devotion. But Melancholy, though an excellent companion for an hour, is the most exacting and depressing of mistresses. The man who gives himself up to her, who always takes too long views, who broods on the future of this planet when the sun has burned out, is on the high-way to madness. The odds are that he does not travel all the way. He remains a self-tormented wretch, highly profitable to his medical man, and a frightful nuisance to his family. Now, there are, of course, cases in which this melancholy has physical causes. It may come of indigestion, and then the remedy is known. Less dining out (indeed, no one will ask the abjectly melancholy man out) and more exercise may be recommended. The melancholy man had better take to angling; it is a contemplative pastime, but he will find it far from a gloomy one. The sounds and sights of nature will revive and relieve him, and, if he is only successful, the weight of a few pounds of fish on his back will make him toss off that burden which poor Christian carried out of the City of Destruction. No man can be melancholy when the south wind blows in spring, when the soft, feathery March-browns flit from the alders and fall in the water, while the surface boils with the heads and tails of trout.

Perhaps, on the other hand, the melancholy one lives too much in the country. Then let him go to Paris or Vienna; let him try the Palais Royal, and spend a good deal of money in the shops. A course of this might have cured even Obermann, whom there was nothing to check or divert while he kept philandering on the mountains with the snows and his woes. There are plenty of such cures for a melancholy not yet incurable; change of air, scene, food, amusement, and occupation being the best. True, the Romans tried this, as Seneca and Lucretius tells us, and found themselves as much bored as ever. "No easier nor no quicker passed th' impracticable hours." But the Romans were very extreme cases.

When the cause of melancholy is religious or moral, there is little to be done with the victim. In "Sartor Resartus" he will read how Mr. Carlyle cured himself, if ever he was cured. To be brief, he said, "What then, who cares?" and indeed, in more reverent form of expression, it is all that can be said. When Nicias addressed the doomed and wasted remnant of the Athenian expedition to Syracuse, he told them that "others, too, being men, had borne things which had to be endured." That is the whole philosophy of the matter.

THACKERAY'S LONDON.

A HOUSE in a highly respectable square, where Jeames Yellowplush was in service, had recently the fame of being haunted. No one knew exactly what haunted this desirable mansion, or how, though a novelist was understood to have supplied a satisfactory legend. The young man who "investigated" the ghost rang the bell thrice violently, and then fell down dead, nor could he in any wise satisfy the curiosity of his friends. That fable is exploded. It was what is called an "ætiological myth;" by the learned it was merely a story devised to account for the fact that the house was not occupied. The imagination of man, confronted by so strange a problem as money running to waste, took refuge in the supernatural. Much more truly haunted than the house in "Buckley Square" are the streets of

London which are tenanted by the ghosts that genius created. These, having never been born, can never die, and still we may meet them in the roads and squares where they lived and took their pastime. Mr. Rideing, an American author, has published (with Messrs. Jarvis and Son) a little volume called "Thackeray's London," an account of the places which that great novelist made household words, and filled with genial spectres that time can never lay. Mr. Rideing's little book does not strike us as being quite complete. Surely Thackeray, especially in the "Ballads," mentions many places not alluded to by the new topographer. Besides, Mr. Rideing says that Thackeray's readers forget the localities in which his characters appear. Surely this is a calumny on human memory. Who but thinks of Becky Sharp as he trudges down Curzon Street? Has Bryanston Square properly any reason for existence, except that the Hobson Newcomes dwelt there? Are the chambers of Captain Costigan forgotten by the memory of any man, or those of Pen and George Warrington? But Pen took better rooms, not so lofty, when he scored that success with "Walter Lorraine."

Where did Mr. Bowes, the hopeless admirer of the Fotheringay, dwell? Every one should know, but that question might puzzle some. Or where was the lair of the Mulligan? Like the grave of Arthur, or of Molière, it is unknown; the whole of the postal district known as W. is haunted by that tremendous shade. "I live there," says he, pointing down towards Uxbridge with the big stick he carries; so his abode is in that direction, at any rate. No more has been given to man to know.

Many minor reminiscences occur to the mind. In Pump Court we encounter the brisk little spectre of Mr. Frederick Minchin, and who can forget that his club was The Oxford and Cambridge, than which what better could he desire? Mr. Thackeray himself was a member of The Garrick, The Athenæum, and The Reform, but the clubs of many of his characters, like the "buth" of Jeames Yellowplush, are "wrapped up in a mistry." They are alluded to by fancy names, but the scholiast on Thackeray will probably be able to identify them. Is it not time, by the way, for that scholiast to give his labours to the public? Thackeray's world is passing; the children he knew, the boys he tipped and took to the play, are middle-aged men—fogies, in fact. *Tempus edax rerum*, Time has an appetite as good as that of a boy at his first club dinner. The meaning of the great writer's contemporary allusions may be lost, like those of Villon and Aristophanes. Such is the fate of comedy. Who knows, if we turn to Dickens, what the "common profeel machine" was, or what were the steps of the dance known as the Fanteag (the spelling is dubious); or what the author meant by a "red-faced Nixon." Was it a nixie? Does the new Professor of the English Language and Literature at Oxford hope to cast the light of Teutonic research on these and similar inquiries? Sam Weller found that oysters always went hand-in-hand with poverty. How this must astonish a generation which finds the oyster nearly as extinct as the ichthyosaurus! The "Book of Snobs" calls aloud for a commentator. Who is the nobleman holding his boots out of the hotel window—an act which the Snob very properly declined to classify as snobbish? Who are the originals of Henry Foker (this, indeed, is known), and of Wagg and Wenham? Or did Wenham's real name *rhyme* to Foker, as, according to the Mulligan,

"Perkins rhymes to Jerkins, my man of firkins"? Posterity will insist on an answer, which will be nothing if not authentic. Posterity, *pace* Mr. Rideing, will remember very well that George Osborne's father lived in Russell Square, and will hunt in vain for 96. There is no such number, any more than there ever was such a Pope as he to whom the unfortunate old woman in "Candid" attributed her birth. Here once more, as Voltaire justly remarks in a footnote, we observe the discretion of our author.

Colonel Newcome lived, as is well known, in Fitzroy Square, and died in the Charter House. To these shrines the pious go in pilgrimage; the rather dingy quarters are brightened by the memory of his presence, as we think of Scott in Castle Street, Edinburgh, or of Dr. John Brown in Princes Street —Dr. John Brown who was a Colonel Newcome that had gone into medicine instead of the army. Smithfield is hardly more memorable for her martyrs than for the battles fought on neighbouring ground between Biggs and Berry, between Cuff and old Figs. Kentish Town, but little sought for sentimental reasons, is glorified by the memory of Adolphus Larkins; "Islington, Pentonville, Somers Town, were the scenes of many of his exploits." Brompton, again, passionate Brompton, lent her shelter—or rather, sold it, for the poetess lived in a boarding-house— to Miss Bunnion. Cursitor Street might be unknown as the great men before Agamemnon (many of whom, by the way, as Meleager and Pirithous, are known well enough) had not Cursitor Street contained the sponging-house where Rawdon Crawley was incarcerated.

In addition to these scholia on Thackeray so sadly needed, and so little likely to be published, we need novelists' maps and topographies of London and Paris. These will probably be constructed by some American of leisure; they order these things better in America. When we go to Paris we want to know where Balzac's men and women lived, Z. Marcas and César Birotteau, and Le Cousin Pons, and Le Père Goriot, and all the duchesses, financiers, scoundrels, journalists, and persons of both sexes and no character "Comédie Humaine." London also might be thus spaced out—the London of Richardson, and Fielding, and Miss Burney, as well as the

London of Thackeray or Dickens. Already, to speak of to-day, Rupert Street is more interesting, because there, fallen in fortune, but resolute of heart and courtly as ever, Prince Florizel of Bohemia held his cigar divan.

TORRID SUMMER.

"Is it very cold?" asks the Prince of Denmark, according to a familiar reading. No one has any occasion to consult the thermometer before answering the question, "Is it very hot?" All things combine to prove that it is very hot. Even the man of metal who used, according to legend, to patrol the coast of Crete, the man with only one vein from head to heel, would admit (could he appear in the Machineries at present) that it is very hot indeed. He might not feel any subjective sensation of heat (for he seems to have been a mythical anticipation of the Conquering Machine which is to dominate the world), but he would have inferred the height of the temperature from a number of phenomena. He would have seen the ticket-clerks in the railway stations with their coats off. He would have observed imitation Japanese parasols at a penny among the ware of enterprising capitalists in the streets. He would have marked the very street-boys in wide, inexpensive straw hats of various and astonishing colours. Woman he would have found in beautiful shades of blue, in such light garments "woven wind" as Theocritus speaks of when he presents the wife of his doctor with a new ivory distaff.

As to men, they in their attire do show their wit or their want of courage, as the case may be. It is not easy for modern man, when he "repairs to the metropolis," to dress up to the heat of the weather. An ingenious though too hasty philosopher once observed that all men who wear velvet coats are atheists. He probably overstated the amount of intellectual and spiritual audacity to be expected from him who, setting the picturesque before the conventional, dons a coat of velvet. But it really does require some originality even to wear a white hat and a white waistcoat in a London July. The heat is never so great but that the majority of males endure black coats and black shiny hats. The others are in a minority. The voice of public opinion is not on their side. "Who stole the moke, Anna?" asked suspicion; and the answer came, "The man in the *chapeau blanc.*" There is something daring, something distinctive in a white hat; and it may be doubted whether the amount of comfort obtained by the revolutionary wearer is in a due ratio to the conspicuousness which his action entails on him. Members of Parliament are singularly emancipated from these fears of the brave; but members of Parliament cannot supply the whole contingent of white-hatted men now to be seen in the streets of the metropolis. Their presence proves that it is very hot indeed. One swallow does not make a summer, but half a dozen pairs of "ducks" beheld in public places would mark a summer of unusually high temperature.

There are, of course, alleviations. Nature compensates all who can afford to purchase the compensations. Strawberries, long waited for, shy, retiring fruit, have now nearly approached the popular price of sixpence a basket. A divine of a past generation declared that in his opinion the joys of Paradise would consist of eating strawberries to the sound of a trumpet. For a poor sixpence half of this transcendental pastime may be partaken of, and probably the brass band which is usually round the corner could supply the sound of the trumpet at a small extra charge.

Unluckily, doctors have decided that many of us must not eat strawberries, nor drink champagne cup, nor iced coffee. That is the way with doctors. Æsculapius was originally worshipped in the form of a serpent; in the guise of a serpent he came to Rome. Medical men still hold of their heroic father, and physicians are the serpents in the Paradise of a warm summer. Mortals, in their hands, are like Sancho Panza with his medical adviser. Here is summer, provoking a gentle interest in every method of assuaging thirst, and almost every method is condemned by one member of the faculty or another. Champagne cannot be so royally sound, nor is shandy-gaff so humble, that it 'scapes whipping. How melancholy a thing is human life at best! In boyhood we can eat more ices than our pocket-money enables us to purchase; in maturity we have the pocket-money without the powers of digestion. The French lady said that if strawberry ices were only sinful, no pleasure could exceed that which is to be enjoyed in the consumption of the congealed fruit. Strawberry ices are sinful now, and under the medical ban. The French lady, were she living still, might be at ease on that score. But her audacity is not given to all, and many fall back on that poor creature, lemon-squash, when they are conscious of a thirst worthy of being quenched by the most imperial beverages in imperial quarts.

Men, being reasonable, must hurry about town when the thermometer is at something fabulous, wearing black clothes, going to parties, and larding the lean earth. Beasts are not so foolish. To the pious Brahmin Vishnu accords the power of becoming what animal he pleases, with a break in the lease, so to speak, when circumstances alter. Had a sage this power at this moment he would become a cow, standing up to her middle in the clear, cool water of the Kennet, under the shade of a hanging willow tree. What bliss can equal that of a cow thus engaged? Her life must, indeed, be burning with a hard gem-like flame. She must be plucking the flower of a series of exquisite moments. The rich, deep grass, with the buttercups and forget-me-nots, is behind her, but she has had enough of that, and is open to more spiritual pleasures. The kingfishers and water-wagtails flit about her. The water-rat jumps into the stream with a soft plash, and his black body scuttles along to the opposite bank. The green dragon-flies float hither and thither; the beautiful frail-winged water-flies float over trout too lazy to snatch at them. The cow, in her sensuous nirvana, may see and marvel at the warm boating-man as he tows two stout young ladies in a heavy boat, or labours with the oar. Her pleasure is far more enduring than that of the bathers in the lasher up stream, and she has an enormous advantage over the contemplative man trying to lie on the grass and enjoy nature, for he really is not enjoying nature. The pleasures of lying on the grass are chiefly those of imagination. You cannot get into a truly comfortable position. Your back has a lump of grass under it here, or your arm tingles and "falls asleep," as children say. No attitude will enable you to read, and the black flies hover around and alight on such of your features as are tempting—to a fly. Then you begin to be quite sure it is damp, and, as you have nothing else to sit on, you sit down on your book, which no one can call comfortable.

The notion of reclining on cushions in a punt is equally fallacious, and, while promising much, ends in a headache. Besides, the river does not always smell very nicely now that it has so long been unrelieved by rain. All through the hot day, in fact, civilized northern man finds loafing very difficult, especially as his Aryan impetuosity is always urging him to do something active. Cows in this climate are the only true lotus-eaters. Next to them in enjoyment comes the angler who approaches the river about eight o'clock, at the time of the "evening rise." He, like the cow, is knee-deep in water, wading; he listens to the plash of big, hungry trout, sucking down gnats under the alders; he casts over them, and if he catches them, who more content than he, as the sky turns from amber to purple and silvery grey, and the light fades till one cannot thread the gut through the eye-hole of one of the new-fashioned hooks? Certainly this man is more blessed than he who is just coming to the ices at a big, hot London dinner, and knows that his physician has forbidden him this form of enjoyment. What a struggle in that person's mind! and how almost predestined is his fall! how sure his repentance next morning!

WESTERN DROLLS.

THE death of Mr. "Josh Billings" may have diminished the stock of harmless pleasures, but can hardly be said to have eclipsed the gaiety of nations. In this country, at least however it may have been in the States, Josh Billings was by no means the favourite or leading American humorist. If phonetic spelling were universal, much of his fun would disappear. His place was nearer that of Orpheus C. Kerr than of Artemus Ward, or of Mark Twain. It has long been the English habit to look for most of our broad fun across the Atlantic. Americans say we are not a funny people. A chivalrous and mediæval French writer, not unfrequently quoted, once made a kindred remark. We are not at present a boisterously comic lot of geniuses, and if you see the tears running down the eyes of a fellow-countryman reading in a railway carriage, if he be writhing with mirth too powerful for expression, the odds are that he has got hold of a Yankee book.

In American country newspapers there is usually one column entirely devoted to facetiæ, which appear to have been clipped out of the columns of other country papers. They live on each other, just as the natives of the Scilly Islands are feigned to eke out a precarious livelihood by taking in each other's washing. It is averred that one American journal, the *Danbury Newsman*, contains nothing but merriment—a fearful idea! We have nothing like this at home, and as for writers who make a reader giggle almost indelicately often, where are they to be found? "Happy Thoughts" affect some of us in this way; others are convulsed by "Vice Versâ;" but, as George Eliot says, nothing is such a strain on the affections as a difference of taste in jokes. It is unsafe to recommend any writer as very funny. No man can ever tell how his neighbour will take a joke. But it may safely be said that authors who really tickle their students are extremely rare in England, except as writers for the stage, and surely "The Great Pink Pearl" might have made Timon of Athens shake his sides, or might convert a Veddah to the belief that "there is something to laugh at." In literature, when we want to be even hysterically diverted, we must, as a rule, buy our fun from the American humorists. If we cannot make laughter ourselves, at least we can, and do, laugh with them.

A vast amount of American humour may be called local and middle-class. In the youth of Dickens, there was a regular set of home-made middle-class jokes about babies, about washing-day, about mothers-in-law, about dinner-parties that were not successes, about curtain lectures, about feminine extravagance in bonnet-buying, about drunken men, about beer, all of them jokes worn threadbare. A similar kind of fun, with local differences, prevails in the States, but is wonderfully mixed up with scriptural and religious jokes. To us sober Britons, whatever our opinions, these latter japes appear more or less ribald, though they are quite innocently made.

Aristophanes, a pious conservative, was always laughing consumedly at the Greek gods, and the Greek gods were supposed to be in the joke. The theatrical season was sacred to the deity of wine and fun, and he, with the other Olympians, was not scandalized by the merriment. In the ages of faith it is also notorious that saints, and even more sacred persons, were habitually buffooned in the Mystery Plays, and the Church saw no harm. The old leaven of American Puritanism has the same kind of familiarity with ideas and words which we approach more delicately, conscious that the place where we tread is holy ground. This consciousness appears to be less present in the States, which are peopled by descendants of the Puritans, and scores of good things are told in "family" American journals and magazines which are received without a grin in this country. "We are not amused," a great person is reported to have once observed when some wit had ventured on a hazardous anecdote. And we, meaning the people of England, are often not amused, but rather vexed, by gaieties which appear absolutely harmless on the other side of the ocean. These two kinds of humour, the middle-class jokes about courting between lovers seated on a snake fence, or about Sunday schools and quaint answers there given to Biblical questions, leave us cold.

But surely we appreciate as well as the Americans themselves the extraordinarily intellectual high spirits of Mark Twain, a writer whose genius goes on mellowing, ripening, widening, and improving at an age when another man would have written himself out. His gravity in narrating the most preposterous tale, his sympathy with every one of his absurdest characters, his microscopic imagination, his vein of seriousness, his contrasts of pathos, his bursts of indignant plain speaking about certain national errors, make Mark Twain an author of the highest merit, and far remote from the mere buffoon. Say the "Jumping Frog" is buffoonery; perhaps it is, but Louis Quinze could not have classed the author among the people he did not love, *les buffons qui ne me font rire*. The man is not to be envied who does not laugh over the ride on "The Genuine Mexican Plug" till he is almost as sore as the equestrian after that adventure. Again, while studying the narrative of how Mark edited an agricultural paper in a country district, a person with any sense of humour is scarcely a responsible being.

He is quite unfit (so doth he revel in laughter uncontrollable) for the society of staid people, and he ought to be ejected from club libraries, where his shouts waken the bald-headed sleepers of these retreats. It is one example of what we have tried to urge, that "Mark's way" is not nearly so acceptable in "The Innocents Abroad," especially when the Innocents get to the Holy Land. We think it in bad taste, for example, to snigger over the Siege of Samaria, and the discomfiture of "shoddy speculators" in curious articles of food during that great leaguer. Recently Mark Twain has shown in his Mississippi sketches, in "Tom Sawyer," and in "Huckle-bury Finn," that he can paint a landscape, that he can describe life, that he can tell a story as well as the very best, and all without losing the gift of laughter. His travel-books are his least excellent; he is happiest at home, in the country of his own Blue Jay.

The contrasts, the energy, the mixture of races in America, the overflowing young life of the continent, doubtless give its humorists the richness of its vein. All over the land men are eternally "swopping stories" at bars, and in the long, endless journeys by railway and steamer. How little, comparatively, the English "swop stories"! The Scotch are almost as much addicted as the Americans to this form of barter, so are the Irish. The Englishman has usually a dignified dread of dropping into his "anecdotage."

The stories thus collected in America are the subsoil of American literary humour, a rich soil in which the plant cultivated by Mark Twain and Mr. Frank Stockton grows with vigour and puts forth fruit and flowers. Mr. Stockton is very unlike Mark Twain: he is quiet, domesticated, the jester of the family circle. Yet he has shown in "Rudder Grange," and in "The Transferred Ghost," very great powers, and a pleasant, dry kind of Amontillado flavour in his fun, which somewhat reminds one of Thackeray—the Thackeray of the "Bedford-row Conspiracy" and of "A Little Dinner at Timmins." Mr. Stockton's vein is a little too connubial—a little too rich in the humours and experiences of young married people. But his fun is rarely strained or artificial, except in the later chapters of "Rudder Grange," and he has a certain kindliness and tenderness not to be always met with in the jester. His angling and hunting pieces are excellent, and so are those of Mr. Charles Dudley Warner. This humorist (like Alceste) was once " funnier than he had supposed," when he sat down with a certain classical author, to study the topography of Epipolæ. But his talent is his own, and very agreeable, though he once so forgot himself as to jest on the Deceased Wife's Sister. When we think of those writers to whom we all owe so much, it would be sheer ingratitude to omit the name of the master of them all, Oliver Wendell Holmes. Here is a wit who is a scholar, and almost a poet, and whose humour is none the less precious for being accompanied by good humour, learning, a wide experience of the world. With Mr. Lowell, he belongs to an older generation, yet reigns among the present. May the reign be long!

SHOW SUNDAY.

THE years bring round very quickly the old familiar events. Yesterday was Show Sunday. It scarcely seems a year since last the painters received their friends, and perhaps a few of their enemies. These visits to studios are very exciting to ladies who have read about studios in novels, and believe that they will find everywhere tawny tiger-skins, Venetian girls, chrysanthemum and hawthorn patterned porcelain, suits of armour, old plate, swords, and guns, and bows, and all the other "properties" of the painter of romance. Some of these delightful things, no doubt, the visitors of yesterday saw, and probably some painters still wear velvet coats and red neckties, and long hair and pointed beards. But the typical artist is not what he was. He has become domesticated. Sometimes he is nearly as rich and "apolaustic" as a successful stockbroker, and much more fashionable. Then he dwells in marble halls, with pleasing fountains, by whose falls all sorts of birds sing madrigals. He has an entirely new house, in short, fitted up in the early Basque style, or after the fashion of an Inca's palace, or like the Royal dwelling of a Rajah, including, of course, all modern improvements. This is a very desirable kind of artist to know at home; but, after all, it is not easy to distinguish him from a highly-cultivated and successful merchant prince, with a taste for *bric-à-brac*. He is not in the least like the painter of romance; perhaps he is better—he is certainly more fortunate; but he is not the real old thing, the Bohemian of Ouida and Miss Braddon. One might as well expect a banker to be a Bohemian.

Another class of modern painter is even more disappointing. He is extremely neat and smooth in his appearance, and dresses in the height of the most quiet fashion. His voice is low and soft, and he never (like the artist of fiction) employs that English word whereby the Royalist sailor was recognized when, attired as a Portuguee, he tried to blow up one of the ships of Admiral

Blake. This new kind of artist avoids studio slang as much as he does long hair and red waistcoats. He might be a young barrister, only he is more polished; or a young doctor, only he is more urbane. No doubt there exist men of the ancient species—rough-and-ready men as strong as bargees, given to much tobacco, amateurs of porter or shandygaff, great hunters of the picturesque, such wild folk as Thackeray knew and Mr. Charles Keene occasionally caricatures. These are the artists whom young ladies want to see, but they are not in great force on Show Sunday. They rather look on that festival as a day of national mourning and humiliation and woe. They do not care to have all Belgravia or South Kensington let loose in their places. They do not wish the public to gaze and simper at pieces which will probably be enskied or rejected, or hung at a dangerous corner next a popular picture.

No painter who is not of the most secure eminence can, perhaps, quite enjoy Show Sunday. Many of his visitors know as much about Art as the Fuegians do of white neckties. They come and gaze, and say, "How soft, how sweet!" like Rosey Mackenzie, and have tea, and go away. Other people offer amazing suggestions, and no one who thinks the pictures failures quite manages to conceal his opinion. Poets are said to be fond of reading their own poems aloud, which seems amazing; but then as they read they cannot see their audience, nor guess how they are boring those sufferers. The poet, like the domestic fowl which did not scream when plucked, is "too much absorbed." But while his friends look at his pictures, the painter looks at their faces, and must make many sad discoveries. Like other artists, he does not care nearly so much for the praise as he is dashed and discomfited by the slightest hint of blame. It is a wonder that irascible painters do not run amuck among their own canvases and their visitors on Show Sunday. That, at least, in Mr. Browning's phrase, is "how it strikes a contemporary." Were the artists to yield to the promptings of their lower nature, were they to hearken to the Old Man within them, fearful massacres would occur in St. John's Wood, and Campden Hill, and round Holland House. An alarmed public and a powerless police would behold vast ladies of wealth, and maidens fair, and wild critics with eye-glasses speeding, at a furious pace, along certain roads, pursued by painters armed to the teeth with palette knives and mahlsticks.

This is what would occur if academicians and others gave way to the natural passions provoked by criticism and general demeanour on Show Sunday. But it is a proof of the triumph of civilization that nothing of this kind occurs. Peace prevails in the street and studio, and at the end of the day the artist must feel much as the critic does after the private view at the Royal Academy. The artist has been having a private view of the public on its good behaviour, and that wild contempt of the bourgeois which burns in every artist's breast must reach its highest temperature. However, the holidays are beginning, the working season is over, and that reflection, doubtless, helps the weary painter through his ordeal. But his friends also have to bear a good deal if they happen not to like his performances. They must feign admiration as well as they may, and the sun of Show Sunday goes down on a world rather glad that it is well over.

Lord Beaconsfield once said at an Academy

dinner that originality was the great characteristic of English art. So little was he supposed to have spoken seriously that another, of whose ceasing to perorate there is no prospect, characterized his criticism in language so strong that it cannot well be repeated. Let us admit that Lord Beaconsfield was either mistaken, or that, like the Consul Aulus, "he spake a bitter jest." Our artists, when they have found their vein, go on working it. They do not wander off in search of new veins, as a general rule. It would be unkind to draw attention to personal proofs of this truism. He who has done well with babies in fancy dresses will go on doing well with infants in masquerade. There are moments when the arrival of Cronus to swallow the whole family of painted babes, as he did his own, would be not unwelcome; when an artistic Herod would be applauded for a general massacre of the Burlington House innocents. But this may be only the jaundiced theory of a jaded critic. The mothers of England are a much more important set of judges, and they like the babies. Then the bishops, though a little monotonous, must be agreeable to their flocks;

while the hunting dogs, and pugs, and kittens, and monks, and Venetian girls—*la blonde et la brune*—and the Highland rivers of the colour of porter "with a head on it," and the mackerel-hued sea, and the marble, and the martyrs, and the Mediterranean—they are all dear to various classes of our teeming population. The critic may say he has seen them all before, he knows them off by heart; but then so does he know Raphael's infants, and Botticelli's madonnas, and Fra Angelico's angel trumpeters, and Vecelli's blue hills, and Robusti's doges, and Lionardo's smiling, enigmatic ladies. He does not say he is tired of these, but that is only his eternal affectation. He is afraid, perhaps, to say that the old masters bore him—that is a compliment reserved for contemporaries. Let it be admitted that in all ages artists have had their grooves, like other men, and have reproduced themselves and their own best effects. But, as this is inevitably true, how careful they should be that the effects are really of permanent value and beauty! Realistic hansom cabs, and babies in strange raiment, and schoolgirls of the last century, and Masters of Hounds, are scarcely of so much permanent value as the favourite types and characters which Lionardo and Carpaccio repeat again and again. We no more think Claude monotonous than we think "the quiet coloured end of evening" flat and stale. But we may, and must, tire of certain modern combinations too often rehearsed, after the trick has become a habit, and the method an open mystery.

THE DRY FLY.

As the Easter vacation approaches, the cockney angler, the "inveterate cockney," as Lord Salisbury did or did not say, begins to look to his fishing tackle. Now comes in the sweet of the year, and we may regret, with Mr. Swinburne, that "such sweet things should be fleet, such fleet things sweet." There are not many days that the London trout-fisher gets by the waterside. The streams worth his attention, and also within his reach, are few, and either preserved so that he cannot approach them, or harried by poachers as well as anglers. How much happier were men in Walton's day who stretched their legs up Tottenham Hill and soon found, in the Lea, trout which would take a worm when the rod was left to fish for itself! In those old days Hackney might be called a fishing village. There was in Walton's later years a writer on fishing named W. Gilbert, "Gent." This gent produced a small work called the "Angler's Delight," and if the angler was delighted, he must have been very easily pleased. The book now sells for large sums, apparently because it is scarce, for it is eminently worthless. The gentle writer, instead of giving directions about fly-dressing, calmly tells his readers to go and buy his flies at a little shop "near Powle's." To the "Angler's Delight" this same W. Gilbert added a tract on "The Hackney River, and the best stands there." Now there are no stands there, except cab-stands, which of course are uninteresting to the angler. Two hundred years have put his fishing far away from him.

However, the ancient longing lives in him, and the Sunday morning trains from Paddington are full of early fishing-men. But it cannot be that most of them are after trout, the Thames trout being so artful that it needs a week's work and private information to come to terms with him. Hitherto he has been spun for chiefly, or coaxed with live bait; but now people think that a good big loch fly may win his affections. It is to be hoped that this view is correct, for the attempts by spinning and with live bait are calculated to stretch and crack even the proverbial patience of anglers. Persons conscious of less enduring mettle in their mind will soon be off to the moorland waters of Devonshire, or the Border, where trout are small, fairly plentiful, and come early into season. About the upper waters of Severn, where Sabrina is still unvexed by pollution, and where the stream is not greater than Tweed at Peebles, sport is fair in spring.

Though the Devonshire, and Border, and probably the Welsh waters, are just in their prime, the season is not yet for the Itchen and the Kennet, with their vast over-educated and over-fed monsters of the deep. Though there may be respectable angling for accomplished artists thereabouts in late April and May, the true sport does not begin till the May-fly comes in, which he generally does in June. Then the Kennet is a lovely and seductive spectacle to the angler. Between the turns of sun and shower the most beautiful delicate insects, frail as gossamer and fair as a fairy, are born, and flit for their hour, and float down the water, soon to be swallowed by the big four-pound trout. He who has no experience of this angling, and who comes to it from practice in the North, at first thinks he cannot go wrong. There is the smooth clear water, broken every moment by a trout's nose, just gently pushed up, but indicating, by the size of the ripple, that a monster is feeding below. You think, if you are accustomed to less experienced fish, that all is well. You throw your flies, two or three, a yard above the ripple, and wait to strike. But the ripples instantly cease, and on the surface of the water you see the long thin track of a broad back and huge dorsal fin. The trout has been, not frightened—he is in no hurry—but disgusted by your clumsy cast, which would readily have taken in a sea-trout or a loch-trout. They of Kennet and Test know a good deal better than to approach your wet flies. A few minutes of this failure reduce the novice to the despair of Tantalus. *He* never was set to such a torture as casting over big feeding trout and never getting a rise. You feel inclined to throw your fly-book bodily at the heads of the trout and bid them take their choice of its contents. That method of angling would be quite as successful as angling for large southern trout in the northern manner. So the novice either loses his temper and walks away to take his ease and some shandy-gaff at the Bear, or he sits down to smoke, or he potters botanically among the flowering water-weeds. Then a southern angler comes near, and is presently playing a trout which the northern man has not "put down," or frightened into total abstinence for the day. Then the true method of fishing for trout in a clear stream is illustrated in practice, and a beautiful and most delicate art it proves to be.

First, the angler notices a rising fish. Then he retires to a safe distance from the bank, outflanks the trout, and comes round in his rear. As fish always feed with their heads up stream, it is necessary in such clear water to fish for them from below, from as far below as possible. Every advantage is taken of cover, and the angler soon acquires the habits of a skirmisher. A tuft of rushes, an inequality in the ground, or an alder bush conceals him; behind this he kneels, and gets his tackle in order. He uses only one fly, not two or three, as people do on the Border. He carefully measures his ground, flicking his cast through the air, so that the fly shall be perfectly dry. Then the trout rises, and in a moment the dry fly descends as lightly as a living insect, half a foot above the ripple. Down it floats, the fisher watching with a beating heart: then there is a ripple, then a splash; the rod bends nearly double, the line flies out to the further bank, and the struggle begins. The fight is by no means over, for the fish instinctively makes for a bed of weeds, where he can entangle and break the line, while the angler holds him as hard as he dares, and, if tackle be sound and luck goes not contrary, the big trout is landed at last.

This is no trifling victory. Nay, a Kennet trout is far harder to catch and kill than the capricious salmon, which will often take a fly, however clumsy be the man who casts it. There is a profane theory that several members of the Hungerford Club never catch the trout they pay so much to have the privilege of trying to capture. A very sure eye and clever hand are needed to make the fly light dry and neat so close above the fish that he has not time to be alarmed by the gut. "Gut-shy" he is, and the less he sees of it the better. Moreover, a wonderful temper is required, for in the backward cast of the long line the hook will, ten to one, catch in a tree, or a flower, or a straw, or a bit of hay, and then it has to be disengaged by the angler crawling on hands and knees. Perhaps a northern angler will never quite master the delicacy of this sport, nor acquire the entomological knowledge which seems to be necessary, nor make up his mind between the partisans of the light one-handed rod and the double-handed rod.

AMATEUR AUTHORS.

LITERATURE knows no Trades Unions, but if things go on as they are at present, perhaps we shall hear of literary rattening and picketing. The *Kölnische Zeitung*, in Germany, has been protesting against the mob of noble ladies who write with ease, though their works, even to persons acquainted with the German tongue, are by no means easy reading. The Teutonic paper requests these ambitious dames to conduct themselves as amateurs, to write, if write they must, but to print only a few copies of their books, and give these few copies only to their friends. This is advice as morally excellent as it will be practically futile, nor does it apply only to ladies of rank, but to amateur novelists in general. The old quarrel between artists and amateurs is fiercely waged in dramatic society, perhaps because actors and actresses feel the stress of competing with cheap amateur labour. Now, though the professional novelist has only of late begun to think seriously of the subject, it is plain that he too is competing with labour unnaturally cheap, and is losing in the competition. To define an amateur is difficult, as all athletic clubs and rowing clubs are aware. But in this particular field of human industry, the amateur may be defined with ease. The amateur novelist is not merely the person who, having another profession, writes a romance by way of "by-work," as the Greeks called it. Lord Beaconsfield was no amateur in romance, and perhaps no novel was ever sold at so high a ransom as "Endymion." Yet Lord Beaconsfield only scribbled in his idle hours, and was not half so much an amateur novelist as Mr. Gladstone is an amateur student of Homer. No; the true amateur is he or she who publishes at his or her own expense. The labour of such persons is not only cheap; its rewards may be estimated by a frightful minus quantity—the publisher's bill. Every one must have observed that when his box of books comes from the circulating library, it by no means contains the books he has asked the librarian to send.

The batch does not exclusively consist of the plums and prizes of the publishing season, of Sir Henry Gordon's book on his illustrious brother, of the most famous novel of the month, of Mr. Romilly's "New Guinea and the Western Pacific"—as diverting a book of travel as ever was written, of Mr. Stockton's "Mrs. Null," and generally of all that is freshest and most notable in biography, fiction, and history. A few of the peaches of the best quality there are, but the rest are fruit less valued, are, in fact, amateur novels. There are two sets of three gaudy novels by unheard-of ladies; and perhaps three shilling novels, with such titles as "Who Did It?" "Chopped in Cover," or "Under a Cloud," none of which names we trust are copyright. A similar phenomenon presents itself at the bookstalls, which are choked with cheap and unenticing brief tales of the deadly sins. And whose fault is it that we do not get the good books and are flooded with the bad books? Why, it is the fault of the ambitious amateur, of the ladies and gentlemen who publish at their own risk, and at the cost of the world of readers and professional writers.

This is, with a few remarkable limitations,

a free country. No law exists which says to publishers, "Thou shalt not publish on commission." No law confines the vagaries of amateur romance. Hence the market is choked, and the circulating libraries are overwhelmed with rubbish, and good books, as the Americans of the West say, "get no show." The debauched novel reader, to whom every story is a story, and one no better nor worse than another, may not heed it, but the judicious grieve, and the artist in fiction returns a smaller income tax. Then the very revenue suffers with the general decline of letters. It may, of course, be urged that all artists are amateurs before they secure a paying public. The amateur novelist may be compared to the young dramatic author who gives his piece at a *matinée*, and who, once in a hundred times, finds a manager to approve it. May not publishing *en amateur* be the only way of reaching the public? To this question the answer is, No! The risk of publishing a novel by a new author is nothing like so great as the risk of producing a play with an unknown name to it. Publishers exist for the purpose of bringing out books that will pay, and they generally pounce on a good manuscript in fiction, whether the writer be known or unknown. It is much more easy to predict whether a novel will pay or not than to prophecy about a drama. Thus the most obscure author (in spite of the difficulties faced by "Jane Eyre" and "Vanity Fair") may rely on it, that if his MS. is not accepted, it is not worth accepting. He should not, if he has decently sound reasons for self-confidence, be disheartened by two or three refusals. One man's taste might be averse to "John Inglesant," another's might turn against Ouida, a third might fail to see the merit of "Vice Versâ." But if half a dozen experts taste and reject a manuscript, it is almost certain to be hopeless. Then the author should take the advice once offered by Mr. Walter Besant. "*Never* publish at your own expense." If you do, you stamp yourself as an amateur; you add to the crowd of futilities that choke the market; and, if you have it in you to write a novel which shall be a good piece, you are handicapping yourself by placing a bad novel on your record. People sin out of thoughtlessness, as well as depravity, and we would not say that every amateur novelist is, *ex officio*, infamous, nefarious, and felonious.

He or she may be only rather vain, conceited, and unreflecting.

Where, then, is the remedy if homilies fail to convert the sinner, as, indeed, it is the misfortune of homilies to fail? The remedy will be found in a Novelists' League, with tickets, and boycotting, and strikes, and rattening, and all the other devices for getting our own way in an oppressive world. There will be a secret society of professionals. Lady novelists (amateurs) will be rattened; their blotting-paper and French dictionaries will be stolen or destroyed; their publishers will be boycotted by all members of the League, who will decline to publish with any man known to deal with amateurs. Nay, so powerful is this dread and even criminal confederacy, that amateurs will not even be reviewed. Neither the slashing, nor the puffing, nor the faintly praising notice will be meted out to them. There will be a conspiracy of silence. The very circulating libraries will be threatened, and coffins (stolen from undertakers who dabble in romance) will be laid at Mr. Mudie's door, unless he casts off the amateur in fiction. The professionals will march through rapine to emancipation. They will strike off the last gyves that fetter the noble art of romance, and in five or six years we shall have only about a tenth of the present number of romances, but that tenth will pass through as many editions as "The Pilgrim's Progress," which, by the way, was probably, like Ronsard's poems, the work of an amateur. But these were other times, when an author did not expect to make money, and thought himself lucky if, after a slashing personal review by the Inquisition, his fragments were not burned at the stake in a bonfire of his volumes.

SOME RARE THINGS FOR SALE.

An American writer has been complaining lately that his countrymen have lost the habit of reading. This is partly the result of that free trade in English books which is the only form of free trade that suits the American Constitution. People do not buy American books any longer, because they can get English works, mere printed rags, but paying nothing to English authors, for a few cents. The rags, of course, fall to pieces, and are tossed into the waste-paper basket, and thus a habit of desultoriness and of abstention from books worth styling books grows and grows, like a noxious and paralysing parasite, over the American intellect. In this way our pleasant vices are made instruments to plague us, and the condition of the law, which leaves the British authors at the mercy of the Aldens and Monros of the States, is beginning to react on the buyers of goods indelicately obtained. Even newspaper articles are becoming, it is said a heavy and a weary weight on the demoralised attention, and people are ceasing to read anything but brief and probably personal paragraphs, such as "Joaquin Miller has had his hair cut."

This is a deplorable condition of things, and perhaps not quite without example at home, where, however, many people still intend to read books, and order them at the libraries, though they never really carry out intentions which, like those of Wilkins Micawber the younger, are excellent. To persons conscious of mental debility and incapable of grappling even with a short shilling novel, a brief and easy form of reading may be recommended. They may study catalogues; they may peruse the lists of their wares which second-hand booksellers and dealers in all kinds of curiosities circulate gratis. This is the only kind of circular which should not go straight to its long home in the waste-paper basket. A catalogue is full of information. It is so exceedingly inconsecutive that even the most successful barrister, or doctor, or stockbroker (they are the people that read least) need not be fatigued by its contents. The catalogue skips from gay to grave, from Tupper to Aretino, from Dickens to "Drelincourt on Death." You can pick it up where you like, and lay it down when your poor fagged attention is distracted by a cab in the street, or a bird in the branches. Then there is the pleasure of marking with a pencil the articles which you would buy if you could—the Nankin double bottle, the old novel bound in the arms of the Comtesse de Verrue, the picture ascribed to the school of Potto Pottoboileri. Of course, in these bad times, such purchases are out of the question, but the taste and judgment are gratified by "marking them down," like partridges in September.

These contemplative reveries on catalogues have been inspired by a catalogue, not without its merits—a list of relics of Mexican history now to be sold. The curious may find it for themselves, the wealthy may speculate in the treasures which it advertises. Here is a piece of the Emperor Maximilian's waistcoat, "same in which they shot him," to employ an idiom of Captain Rawdon Crawley's. There are many relics of the same recent and troublous times; but the amateur is more strongly attracted by a very singular series of objects of the times of the Spanish Conquest, nearly four hundred years ago. It is not so much the obsidian idols, made of that curious bottle-glass-like mineral so fashionable among the Aztecs, as the authentic remains of Fernando Cortes that the collector will covet. What man had ever such fortune as Cortes—he who discovered a new world as strange as a new planet? He conquered a great civilized race, he overthrew a dynasty, not only of mortals, but of gods. Huitzilopochtli and Quetzalcoatl fled from him, and their hideous priests, draped and masked in skins fresh flayed from beasts or men, vanished at his coming, as Isis, Osiris, and the dog Anubis fled from the folding star of Bethlehem. He fought battles like the visions of romance, and he took great and stately cities, with all their temples and towers, which a month before were as unknown to Europeans as the capitals of Mars and Sirius. The wonderful catalogue of which we speak is rich in relics of this hero. We are offered a chance to buy his "trunk," a carved wooden trunk in which Cortes carried his personal property. His army chest, which held the sacred gold of Montesuma and the treasure of the Temple of the Sun, is to be sold for a consideration. His pistols are also on sale, and his "field-glass," which must be an exceedingly early example of that useful invention. Whether the field-glass is binocular or not, the catalogue does not pause to inform us. Corslets worn by his brave Castilians are also to be vended, perhaps the very leather and steel that guarded the honest heart of good Bernal Diaz. But all these treasures, and even the very "scissors" of Fernando Cortes, are less enticingly romantic than the iron head of Alvarado's spear. Surely no spear since that of Peleus' son, not to be wielded by meaner men, has ever been so well worth acquiring as the spear of Alvarado, Tonatrish the sun-god, as he was called by the Mexicans, by reason of his long, bright, golden hair. This may have been, probably was, the spear that Alvarado bore when he charged up the steps of the great Teocalli or God's house, rained upon by Aztec darts, driving before him the hordes of heathendom. With this very spear, when the summit was gained, he may have fought in that strange fight, high in air, beheld by all the people of the city and all the allies of Spain. Here stood the Christian cross; there was planted the war-god, Huitzilopochtli; there the two faiths fought out their battle, and the vanquished were tossed dying down the sides of the Teocalli. Then the Spaniard was victorious; fire was set to the Teocalli, and the cannibal Aztec religion rolled away in the clouds of smoke and vapour of flame. With the self-same spear (no doubt) did Alvarado make his famous leap, using it as a leaping pole to clear the canal during the retreat of the Night of Dread. Assuredly Alvarado's spear, or even the iron head of it alone, is an object worthy of an archæologist's regard, and scarce less curious than that

> "Broomstick o' the Witch of Endor,
> Weel shod wi' brass,"

which Burns describes in the collection of Captain Grove. But extraordinary as is the charm of these relics of Anahuac and of Castille, perhaps even more engrossing is the last article in this romantic catalogue, namely, "a green portfolio" giving an account of the various articles, and how they came into the hands of their proprietor. Their pedigree, if authentic, must be most important.

Probably the most inattentive mind, even in the holidays, could "tackle" a catalogue like this, or another in which the snuff-box of Xerxes and the boot-jack of Themistocles should be offered for sale. These antiquities seem scarcely less desirable, or less likely to come into the market, than the scissors, pistols, and field-glass of Fernando Cortes. An original portion of the Tables of the Law (broken on a familiar occasion by the prophet), Hannibal's cigarette case, a landing net (at one time in the possession of Alcibiades), a piece of chalk used by Archimedes in his mathematical demonstrations, the bronze shoe of Empedocles, the arrow on which Abaris flew, and the walking-stick, a considerable piece of timber, which Dr. Johnson lost in Mull, may all be reposing in some private collection. Collectors do get very odd things together. Poor M. Soleirol had quite a gallery of portraits and autographs of Molière, and a French mathematician, about a dozen years ago, possessed an assortment of apocryphal letters from almost every one mentioned in history, sacred or profane. The collection of Mr. Samuel Ireland was like this, and an English student possessed autographs of most of the great reformers, carefully written by an ingenious swindler in contemporary books. The lovers of relics are apt to be thus deluded, and perhaps we should not regret this, as long as they are happy. But they should be very careful indeed when they are asked to buy Alvarado's spear, though probably it is extant somewhere, as it certainly is in the catalogue. It is a question of caution in the purchaser.

CURIOSITY HUNTING.

WHAT will people not collect in this curious age, and what prices will they not pay for things apparently valueless? Few objects can seem less desirable than an old postage-stamp, yet our Paris correspondent informs us that postage-stamps are at a premium in the capital of taste and of pleasure. A well-known dealer offers £4 15s. for every Tuscan stamp earlier than 1860, and £16 for particularly fine examples. Mauritius stamps of 1847 are estimated—by the purchaser, mind—at two thousand francs, and post-marks of British Guiana of 1836, from five hundred to a thousand francs. Eighty pounds for a soiled bit of paper, that has no beauty to recommend it! Probably no drawing of equal size from the very hand of Raffaelle or Leonardo would be priced nearly so high as these grubby old stamps. Yet the drawing would be not only a thing of art, beautiful in itself, but also a personal relic of the famous artist whose pencil touched it, while a stamp is a relic of nothing but some forgotten postal arrangement with a colony. We do not know, moreover, how much the dealer will ask for these stamps when once he gets hold of them and has rich collectors at his mercy. In no trade do the buyer's price and the seller's price differ with such wide margins as in the commerce of curiosities, especially, perhaps, in the book-trade. People find that they possess books highly priced in dealers' catalogues, and, if they want money, they carry their treasures to the dealers. But "advantage seldom comes of it." The dealer has a different price, very often, when he is a purchaser. This is intelligible, but, to many persons who are not amateurs, the mania for rare postage-stamps passes all understanding. Yet it is capable of being explained. Like many other oddities and puzzling features in the ways of collectors, the high price of certain stamps is the consequence of the passion for perfection. Any one can collect stamps—little boys and schoolgirls often do. But there comes a point at which foreign stamps and old stamps grow rare, and more rare, and, finally, next to impossible to procure. Here it is that the heart of the mature collector begins to beat. He is determined to have a perfect collection. Nothing shall escape him in the way of printed franks on letters. Now, nineteen-twentieths of his assortment he can buy in the gross, without trouble or great expense; but the last twentieth demands personal care and attention, and the hunting up of old family letters, and the haunting of great dealers' shops, and peeping through dirty windows in shady lanes and alleys. As he gets nearer and nearer a complete collection the spoil grows more and more shy, the excitement faster and more furious, till, finally, the amateur would sell an estate for a square inch of paper, and turn large England to a little stamp, if he had the opportunity. The fury of the pastime is caused by the presence of definite limits. There is only a certain known number of stamps in the world. This limit makes perfection possible.

It is not as if you were collecting really beautiful things like Tanagra terra-cottas, or really rare and quaint and mysterious things like aggery beads. Though Tanagra terra-cottas, and aggery beads, and fine examples of Moorish lustre, or of ancient Nankin, or of gold coins of the Roman Empire, are all rare, yet there is no definite limit to their number. More may turn up any day when the pickaxe breaks into a new Tanagra cemetery, when a fallen palm in Ashanti brings up aggery beads clinging to its earthy roots, when a pot of coins is found by some old Roman way, and so forth. To be sure, perfection may be attained in coin collecting, when a man has specimens of all known sorts, but even then he will pine for better specimens, for the best specimens. In the other branches of the sport we have mentioned the collector may be eager, of course, for good things, but he can never know the passion of the stampomaniac who has all sorts but three, and finds these within his reach. Perfection is within a step of such a man, and that step we fear he will take, even if it involves ever so many breaches of the Decalogue. In one of this month's magazines, in a story called "Mr. Pierrepoint's Repentance," Mr. Grant Allen tells the tale of a coin collector's infamy, and that coin collector a clergyman and fellow of his college.

A pope is said to have stolen a rare book from a painter, and it is certain that enthusiastic collectors are apt to have "their moral tone lowered some," as the American gentleman said about the lady whom he had wooed with intentions less than honourable.

A good example of the toils of the collector in pursuit of perfection is given by M. Henri Beraldi in his very amusing catalogue of M. Paillet's library. This book, by the way, is itself scarce, and the bibliomaniac will be rather lucky if he meets with it. M. Beraldi describes M. Paillet's copy of Dorat's "Fables," published in 1773, with illustrations by Marillier. Nobody perhaps ever reads Dorat now, but his book came out in the very palmiest days of the art of illustration in France. There were no *photogravures* then, nor hideous, scratchy, and seamy "processes," such as almost make one despair of progress and of the future of humanity. The people that takes to "processes" is lost! The illustrations of the "Fables" were duly engraved on copper. There were ninety-nine vignettes, and as many tail-pieces. The bibliographical history of the book is instructive, either to young collectors or to the common herd, not to speak impolitely—the persons who do not understand what collectors want. The "Fables" were originally published on three different sorts of paper, Dutch paper at seventy-two francs, French paper at twenty-nine francs, and on "small paper" at twenty-four francs. In 1853 the original drawings were bought by one of the Rothschilds for about £60; they would now, probably, be worth at least £1,000. The ordinary copies of the book itself bring about £6, the large paper copies about £30, and a copy in old morocco can hardly be estimated—you may pay anything for it, as a copy in old calf has sold for £240.

Such is the natural history of a book pretty valueless as literature, the "Fables" of Dorat. In the early edition of "Brunet's Manual," published in 1821, the large paper copies of the work, with the engravings in the earliest state, are priced at from fifteen to eighteen francs. These vignettes had gone out of fashion; they have come in again with a vengeance. The high prices, eighty or a hundred pounds, are merely the beginning of what the great collectors are ready to pay, and to do, and to suffer in the cause of Dorat. In M.

Cohen's catalogue of all these old illustrated books special mention is made of M. Paillet's copy of the "Fables." It is "a superb example, with all the engravings printed separately." But M. Paillet describes this specimen far more lovingly. All the designs are separately printed, and, oh joy! all have all their margins uncut. The book is "all that man can dream of" in the way of perfection. Cuzin did the binding, in yellow morocco, tooled with roses and butterflies. "Reader," cries M. Beraldi, "if you are not a collector you cannot imagine the difficulty of getting such a copy. It is the thirteenth labour of Hercules." First you buy your text, then you must have the separately printed *fleurons*. These can only be picked up here and there, in sales and stalls. Perhaps you purchase half of them in one lucky investment. With no great difficulty you secure another lot. Then begins the hunt—you buy assortments at the price of bank notes, merely for the sake of two or three out of the mass. You offer to barter twenty-five for one you have not got. Then you have all but three, which you demand from the universe at large ; then all but two; then all but one. What you pay for that one you keep a profound secret, lest your family should have you put under control. Even then you are not safe, for some of your engravings have false margins, and must be changed for entire examples. Such are the joys of the collector, for shadows we are and engravings *à toutes marges* we pursue.

THE END.

PRINTED BY WILLIAM CLOWES AND SONS, LIMITED,
LONDON AND BECCLES.

www.ingramcontent.com/pod-product-compliance
Lightning Source LLC
Chambersburg PA
CBHW021830230426
43669CB00008B/929